THE BEGINNER'S GUIDE TO PICKLING & FERMENTING

Learn The Secrets Of Pickling And Fermenting With Over 1000 Days Worth Of Easy, Nutrient Dense Recipes And Many Tips & Tricks That Will Make You A Pro

Dorothy J. Morgan

Table of Contents

Introduction

Fermenting and pickling are ancient techniques that have been used for centuries to improve food quality by adding probiotic bacteria. If you have never heard of fermentation and pickling, you will soon learn about its marvels. If you are new to fermenting and pickling, you can use this book as your guide. This book has all the information you need about these methods. It introduces the concept of fermenting and pickling and its benefits.

These recipes are simple and give you the right quantities of ingredients you need to use. Although people have always consumed fermented foods, it is only recently that awareness of this cuisine category has increased. Fermenting is a hot new trend in modern food. Not only does it make dishes taste better, but it's also good for you! This cookbook is an amazing resource for the beginner fermenter and the seasoned expert, containing all of the basic information and recipes you will need to jump into this fascinating world headfirst. Learn how easy it is to create your own sauerkraut at home, as well as kimchi and pickles. Discover the amazing health benefits of fermented foods with delicious recipes.

Learn about the tools and ingredients you need, where to source them, and how to ensure you have everything you need for successful fermenting. Your bread, salami, beer, and other foods are all fermented. They are all wonderful additions to your diet, and each has distinctive tastes and sensations. Making your own probiotics at home is a great idea because they are beneficial to your health. As you read this book, you can prepare the greatest fermented foods using the straightforward recipes provided. Every dish has variants that should satisfy every palate.

Another popular method of food preservation for countless generations has been pickling. According to historical studies, pickling has been practiced for at least three thousand years and possibly longer, with its origins in ancient Greece and Egypt. Pickling was valued even then for its nutritional benefits and for enhancing the physical appearance of those who devoured it, and it's used as a food preservation technique. The pickle has developed into a craft with flavors ranging from basic to sophisticated over the ages, creating a prized meal that is now cherished for its culinary excellence and health-improving qualities.

We must first dispel the myth that cucumbers are the only vegetables that may be pickled when discussing pickling today. When it comes to pickling, the possibilities are virtually endless, and the technique may be used on a staggering variety of fruits, vegetables, meats, and even eggs. You may find some of the best and easiest pickling recipes for a wide range of foods in this book. Additionally, you will discover various pickling techniques. Your intended use and the amount of time you choose to spend on your pickles will have a major impact on your chosen method. You're about to learn how extremely simple, pleasurable, and fulfilling creating your own pickles can be, regardless of your pickling technique. All you need is a fundamental understanding of the advantages, resources, and ingredients, which are all covered in this book. To enjoy and share with your family and friends, a cornucopia of freshly pickled crisp vegetables and exquisite fruits is waiting for you.

Pickling and Fermenting as Preservation

Pickling is preserved in vinegar or brine. The process is an old one, but it has become widespread and more common in recent years, with a worldwide growth rate of about 3% every year. Although the popularity of pickles is not yet rivaling that of tomatoes as an agricultural crop, there are still a lot of people who enjoy them. Pickles have been described as "the soul of summer" because they make for such a refreshing snack with the heat wave finally breaking around you! Pickled items like cucumbers, gherkins, and cauliflower florets can be enjoyed raw or on salads, while other pickles like dill spears and apples are best served warm with cream cheese or peanut butter. Hot dogs and hamburgers are not complete without chopped pickles! Tater tots, pot roast, jarred beets, deviled eggs, and potato salad can also make use of pickled items as a flavorful addition that boosts the experience.

Pickling is also said to be effective in controlling disease vectors such as mosquitoes and cockroaches by limiting their food supply. This is because the acidic environment in which the pickle is stored is unappealing to them. It has been found that cucumbers are especially effective in repelling bacteria when they are pickled while cauliflower florets have an overwhelmingly positive effect on termite control. Pickles can be put up as a side dish with meats and soups or used to ramp up the main dish by adding grated cucumbers in place of bread crumbs. They are useful in making cheesecakes because they don't melt no matter how long they are cooked. There's even a strain of pickles known as the "Giant Pickle," which is an excellent side dish to any meal due to its size and structure. The salty and acidic taste of pickles complements most dishes already, so it's not surprising that they are so sought after. Pickles can also be used as a flavoring agent in the form of simple syrup or brine that is used to marinate meats and vegetables. In this way, they may not always preserve the original flavor of an ingredient, but they add their own unique touch and texture to whatever they're added to. Pickles also come in handy when you have too much of one ingredient left over after making another dish. Nothing is wasted! An excess amount of breadcrumbs, for example, can be processed into bread and butter pickles, while cucumber slices can be turned into sweet dill pickles given the right ingredients.

Fermentation, on the other hand, has been used since as early as 4000 BC and was used to preserve wine before the advent of refrigeration by fermentation into vinegar (which would not spoil). After gas cylinders became commercially viable, traditional fermentation methods were replaced with industrial-scale production. Currently, however, with better preservation techniques at our disposal and a lack of demand for handcrafted goods in general, there has been a revival in the local production of fermented foods and beverages.

What Is Picking?

People often confuse the word "pickling" with "canning." While these are both words used to describe preserving food, they mean different things. Pickling is a preservation method that involves submerging raw vegetables or fruit in a brine (salt water) or vinegar mixture and then keeping them stored in the fridge. On the other hand, canning is a type of food preservation where glass jars are filled with raw vegetables and then boiled in water for many hours.

Pickles aren't only salty and sour though, so don't be afraid of trying new flavors! You can make exotic pickles like mango and ginger or even sweet pickles, which are really delicious on burgers. Another thing that people often ask is how soon they can eat the pickles after they're made. If you've done the proper process, then the pickles are safe to eat right away! Pickles can be stored anywhere from a week to a year (or more), and they're still good as long as they haven't spoiled.

Pickling is an ancient food preservation method that has been around for thousands of years. In ancient Egypt, amphorae were used to store fruits and vegetables in brines or oils and were allowed to ferment for months at a time, creating a tangy flavor. In fact, this method is so effective that it's still practiced today in many parts of the world. In present-day times, vegetables are often not fermented at all, but instead are preserved with vinegar or brine. This method is called "brining" and typically involves submerging the vegetables in a salty solution. When properly done, this reduces discoloration as well as increases the shelf life of the pickles by removing oxygen from the juice.

Brine also provides a way to make pickles without having to use any alcohol or fermenting agents like yeast or bacteria. There are a lot of traditions and methods for making pickles, such as the use of special glass jars, the use of spices and meats to flavor the pickles, and even chilies (cayenne pepper is usually used in vinegar pickles). There are also many different types of recipes for pickles, from dill to sweet. The simplest recipe uses just salt, water, and a little vinegar!

Difference Between Quick Pickles and Fresh Pickles

When comparing quick pickles and fresh pickles, there are many differences that stand out. Namely, the time it takes for each kind of dill to become crisp when fermented. As a result of this, there are many different factors influencing the quality and taste of your pickle. Before we get into the differences between quick pickles and fresh pickles, it's first important to understand some of the basic processes that are required for both kinds of pickles.

Preparing Quick Pickles Time: 5 to 7 Days

Quick pickling recipes call for an initial brine in which a vinegar base is mixed with other ingredients such as spices, sugar, and salt. When properly fermented, the brine turns into a crisp brined product. This process takes between 5 to 7 days to ferment and then needs to be processed. If you want to be sure your pickle is ready for consumption before a long wait, you can add nitrite or use canning methods (which are listed later).

Preparing Fresh Pickles Time: 2 to 3 Weeks

Fresh pickling recipes call for adding vegetables or fruits to a vinegar base without any additional ingredients. The recipe also requires fermentation as well as a brining process to achieve the desired taste and texture. Therefore, this process can take between 2 to 3 weeks to complete. When finished, the pickle is usually stored in a refrigerator or freezer.

Quick pickling recipes include vinegar and spices such as garlic, onions, mustard seeds, cayenne pepper, and turmeric. These spices are added to vinegar and salt for a preliminary brining process. Applying these spices is meant to soften the vegetables and help the pickling process. After the vegetables are softened in this manner, they can be either processed or canned. Both canned and quick pickles may be stored for months at a time. The fermenting process for fresh pickles is similar to that of quick pickles, except that it does not include any spices or ingredients. Instead, fresh pickles are kept submerged in cold water, which contributes to the fermentation process.

Quick pickles are crunchy and have a flavorful crispness that lasts for months. They taste similar to a fresh pickle but do not require constantly eating fresh vegetables. This factor makes quick pickles a great alternative to fresh produce options. They are not ideal for those looking to cut calories or fat, as they are high in saturated fat content. Furthermore, they tend to contain more salt than the recommended daily allowance. However, these factors can be controlled when canned efficiently and processed properly.

Fruits and vegetables picked at different times will ferment at different speeds. The quicker the vegetable or fruit is picked, the faster it will ferment. There are several factors that influence this, one of which is the actual ambient temperature of the ingredients and their proximity to light. Fruits that tend to grow in sunny areas will ferment faster than those that grow under shady trees and bushes. This is due to the changing conditions, such as warmer days leading to increased fermentation resulting in a mild pickle product. On the other hand, vegetables can be more affected by high temperatures compared to fruits. This is because they have a shorter ripening period before harvest compared to fruits. This means that these vegetables will be harvested at a time when the brining process has already been completed. Note that this will result in a quicker fermenting period compared to if they were harvested after the fermentation process has already begun. This is just one of many factors influencing the speed of fermenting.

The flavor of quick pickles and fresh pickles are also two different things. This is mainly due to the differing types and amounts of spices used in each kind of pickling recipe. Some quick pickles, such as French jams and marmalades, rely heavily on spices to add flavor, while others, like those made of corn, vegetables, and fruits, use fewer spices in comparison to their other counterparts, which are mostly used for baking instead.

Quick pickles tend to have a higher rate of pickle brine, vinegar, or sugar content. This results in the pickle being sweeter in taste than those that were fermented for longer periods of time. On the other hand, quick pickles made from fruits and vegetables that contain higher amounts of natural sugar may not need additional sweeteners at all. These include fruits like mangoes and pears and vegetables such as cucumbers and cabbage. The ability to alter the quality and taste of your fresh or quick pickles requires you to look at each farm individually. The closer you live to each farm or vegetable supplier, the fresher your produce will be when you consume it. Use these tips to increase the likelihood of getting a good quality pickle or preserve.

When buying your vegetables, make sure you're buying freshly picked ones instead of those that have been sitting in the refrigerator for several days or weeks. A good tip is to stock up on a few bags at once and freeze them immediately for later consumption. Then, when you want fresh vegetables for your family, pull out the freezer bags and cook with the vegetables as if they were fresh from the farm. This trick will ensure you get a better taste from your fresh produce.

What Is Fermenting?

Fermentation is a chemical process that takes advantage of microorganisms to break down organic compounds. The process typically converts carbohydrates to alcohols or organic acids and produces heat or carbon dioxide as a by-product. Microorganisms are bacteria and yeasts in fermentation, but they can also include any other organisms (like fungi) that help with the fermenting process. This is why many types of foods are fermented (such as cheese, yogurt, and soy sauce). Fermentation occurs when microorganisms interact with sugar molecules in foods and make them into other substances, such as carbon dioxide or organic acids like lactic acid. Fermentation can be helpful to food preservation because harmful microorganisms cannot grow in acidic environments. Unfortunately, many bacteria can survive (including some beneficial probiotic bacteria). Bacterial fermentation converts sugars and carbohydrates into acidic products like lactic acid.

Some foods, such as wine and yogurt, involve fermentation to give them their distinct flavor and taste. Wine is made by the alcoholic fermentation of a solution of sugar (usually grape juice) with yeast. Yogurt is a product that involves bacterial fermentation; it is made when milk sours due to the action of microorganisms like lactobacillus bulgaricus and streptococcus thermophilus. Many fruits or vegetables begin as sugar molecules that can be manipulated through bacterial or fungal action during natural processes like dehydration and exposure to air. This process is why many fruits and veggies are very mushy when you buy them. Those sugars are converted through bacterial and fungal action into complex organic acids, alcohols, esters, ketones, and aldehydes. The chemical reaction produces heat. Hot peppers have capsaicin in their cells that cause the burning sensation on your tongue, all due to those bacteria! The pepper's heat is caused by a chemical reaction that occurs during fermentation.

Fermentation occurs in the environment of the food and in the digestive tract of animals as they eat food. Some microorganisms, such as yeast and lactobacillus, are plant-like organisms, while others, such as bacteria and yeasts, are animal-like organisms. They all have strings of genetic material called chromosomes that contain the information to make proteins that allow them to live and reproduce. Every cell in your body has similar DNA to bacteria and yeasts. Another way for microorganisms to help with fermentation is through the aid of a special enzyme called maltase. The enzyme maltase breaks down starch into sugars that can be used by microorganisms during fermentation reactions.

BENEFITS OF FERMENTATION

Fermentation gives us a number of different benefits. It preserves foods that would not otherwise last long on store shelves or in the refrigerator; it gives us the opportunity to grow or produce foods in areas where growing them is not possible. It helps to improve flavor and nutrition by adding minerals and vitamins, and by changing a food's structure into a more nutritious substance. Fermentation also increases the digestibility of these foods as well as enhances their taste, making them more desirable. It also provides health benefits, with some fermented foods offering higher nutritional value than raw vegetables.

Fermented foods often have a low G.I. value; that is, they are low in calories but high in nutrients. Polysaccharides (carbohydrates made up of long chains of sugars) are fermented by bacteria, forming short-chain fatty acids such as acetic acid and lactic acid. Fruits and vegetables that contain polysaccharides, such as grains, beans, and root vegetables, are typically high in polysaccharide content, and thus fermented foods offer an abundance of necessary vitamins, minerals, and other nutrients.

The fermentation process is used for foods that are otherwise not possible to grow or produce in certain parts of the world. For example, wine is made from grapes that you cannot grow in an area if you do not have the right temperature or soil. You can also ferment foods to make them have a higher concentration of nutrients like vitamin C or protein. For example, sauerkraut is made by fermenting cabbage with salt, which causes lactic acid bacteria to break down the pectin and soften the cabbage leaves. This process makes it easier for your body to digest and absorb nutrients from the food (i.e., vitamin C). Eggs are also made more digestible by the fermentation process as well. As always, fresh, whole foods and healthy eating habits are best for you and your family.

Many cultures have enjoyed fermented foods for centuries because they add flavor to meals and were often the only way that foods could be stored before the invention of refrigeration. In many countries, such as India, fermented milk is a part of daily meals and provides protein for communities that depend on milk from cattle. Yogurt is a great source of calcium in countries like Bulgaria, where drinking milk is not a common practice.

Planning Your Fermentation Project

Fermenting at home is an exciting and liberating endeavor. It's also a little complicated. When you start, you have a lot to think about, like what you'll need to get started, the process of fermentation, how to ensure success, and avoid the dreaded yeast and bacteria blooms. Should you use it for baking, smoothies, or soup? The possibilities are endless. There's also the equipment. Here are some things you'll need to ferment at home:

STARTER CULTURES

You can either purchase or make your own starter cultures. Some yeast and bacteria are naturally occurring in the air, so if you're fermenting in a warm place, they may already be present in fruits or vegetables. However, there's no guarantee that these wild airborne organisms will be good quality or that they will thrive with your chosen food. These have been imported from cultures that have been tested time and time again. Fermentation racks are also a great way to store your equipment, allowing you to find the right tool for the job right when you need it instead of searching around for it later. If you're making kombucha, for instance, you need a fermentation vessel that is designed for brewing. A large keg is ideal. You can anchor your fermenting bucket or crock with bungee cords to the bar, then place a wire rack on top of it so you can easily reach your tools when they're needed during fermentation.

CONTAINER

You'll need a container to hold your ferment. While you can use anything from a vase to a storage jar, it's best to start small on your first project. The containers should be made of food-grade plastic or glass and should be free of cracks or scratches.

FERMENTATION WEIGHTS

Another handy product that will make your job easier is the fermentation weight, which is basically a plate that fits perfectly over the top of whatever you're fermenting so that the ingredients are submerged in the liquid below them. This ensures an even and consistent atmosphere throughout the mass to prevent yeast or bacteria blooms and other problems you might encounter during fermentation.

STERILE CONTAINERS

Nothing less than 100% sterile and odorless containers should be used, especially when you're working with fruit or vegetables. These are also great ideas if you're working with ingredients that may be harboring bacteria without your knowledge. Fill the container to the top with water and add one cup of bleach per gallon of water. Soak the fruit or vegetables for 20 minutes, then rinse and rinse again until the rinse water runs clear. Bacteria will get trapped in any remaining nooks or crannies, so cleaning your tools is just as important as cleaning your food or equipment before using it for fermentation. If you have a lot of food to ferment, you'll need a lot of containers. Soak the fermentation jars in hot water to heat up the contents, then rinse them out thoroughly before use. Never use plastic storage containers for fermenting food as they aren't airtight — they'll create an environment that will encourage mold to grow.

A THERMOMETER

Keeping an eye on the temperature of your ferment can help you prevent one of the most common problems encountered during fermentation: yeast, bacteria, and mold from growing too rapidly. If you're working with liquids that are higher than 80°F (27°C), you'll need a thermometer to monitor temperature and gauge when bacteria should be skimmed off or moved into a new container.

CHEESECLOTH

Cheesecloth is a great way to strain liquids without getting all tangled up in complicated tools. Soak your cheesecloth in water, wring it out and use it to line the strainer you're using to strain liquids out of your ferment.

A PRESSURE COOKER

If you're working with liquids that are higher than 118°F (48°C), you'll need to process them in a pressure cooker. Pressure cookers aren't just for beans and peas anymore! They trap juice and flavor in whatever you're cooking so that it doesn't evaporate or get lost during the boiling process. This is an especially good idea if you're working with vegetables that are tough to break down or make stringy, like asparagus.

A COLLECTION VESSEL

This can be anything from a crock to a jar, though it's best to use glass or stainless steel whenever possible. If the container is airtight, it will help keep mold and mildew at bay in case you need to store your ferment for any length of time.

YEAST REHYDRATION

Rehydrating yeast gives it time to wake up and expand without drying out completely so that it has time to react with whatever you're fermenting and absorb flavor, which in turn makes the flavor stronger. You can do this by leaving the yeast out in the water that's room temperature. You'll want to keep the yeast covered with a little bit of moisture at all times.

SWEETENERS

Depending on what you are making, you may want to use sweeteners and/or spices to help enhance the flavor. Use as much as necessary depending on what you're making, but don't overdo it—too much sugar will make your finished product taste overly sugary or sickly sweet.

MULTI-PURPOSE CLEANER & SANITIZER

It's important that any tools used during fermentation are sanitized before and after going into the fermenting vessel so that bad microbes can't spread from one place to another.

METAL CANNING RACK

A metal canning rack makes it easy to place your fermenting containers into the fermenting vessel during fermentation. You can secure the container in place with a bungee cord (recommended) or by placing a cork in the lid, which will prevent excess gas from escaping.

FERMENTATION VESSEL

Once you're certain that you have everything you need, you can begin fermentation. If you have an empty vase or jar, fill it with water to use as your fermentation container. Make sure that it's not too deep so that the bacteria can still breathe, then put your fermented food ingredients in the water and secure them with a weight placed over the top of them, so they stay submerged throughout the fermentation process.

Place the food ingredients in your fermenting vessel and secure them with the weight you chose. If you're using a jar, fill it to the brim with water, then place your fermenting container inside. If you're using a vase, fill it with water as well and pour it into the fermenting vessel, then secure the fermenting container with a weight over the top of it to keep moisture and bacteria from escaping during fermentation. Place a thermometer in the fermenting vessel to monitor temperature throughout the process. While you're monitoring temperature, make sure it doesn't rise above 80°F (27°C). If it does, you'll have to transfer your food ingredients into a new fermenting vessel before they get too hot and start to spoil.

Add 1 tablespoon of sea salt to your fermenting vessel (if the liquid is higher than 90°F or 32°C) and set aside for 24 hours. This is optional, but it will help keep bacteria from developing during fermentation. After 24 hours, place the food ingredients into a cheesecloth bag and secure it with a rubber band or string. Leave the food ingredients in the fermenting container and secure it with the weight on top of it.

After 5 to 7 days, you'll notice that your fermenting jar is bubbling and fizzing, which means that you have a healthy environment for fermentation to take place. At this point, it's time to remove your fermenting jar from the vessel and transfer your fermented food ingredients into a new one. As soon as you can, remove your now-milder food ingredients from their bag and place them in an airtight container.

Store your fermented food in a cool, dark place or refrigerate at this point. The ideal temperature for storing ferments is between 50 and 65° F (10 to 18° C). Harvest your vegetables after 5 days and enjoy the fruit of your labor! You'll find that they are slightly sour, but that their flavor will continue to develop in the coming days and weeks.

FERMENTING RECIPES

1. Basic Cabbage Sauerkraut

Preparation Time: 10 minutes
Cooking Time: 5 minutes

INGREDIENTS:

- 3 lb thinly shredded green cabbage (from about 3 small heads)
- 1 ½ tbsp Diamond Crystal kosher salt

DIRECTION:

1. Place shredded cabbage in a very large bowl. Sprinkle salt all over the cabbage. Massage or pound cabbage, making sure salt goes everywhere. You can use your hands or a cabbage pounder (a large wooden muddler) to do this. Wear gloves if you have cuts or sensitive hands. As you massage cabbage, you will start to see and feel it become softer and notice some water. You should get thc cabbage to a point where you can pick up a handful and squeeze liquid from it. I's will take 10 to 20 minutes.
2. Pack the cabbage into a quart jar, including juice, and pack it down, eliminating any air pockets you can find. Cabbage should be packed down so much that juices should start to come up over cabbage.
3. Once the cabbage has been packed down with brine covering the top of it, place a weight on it to keep the cabbage submerged in the brine. If using a crock, use crock weight; if using a Mason jar, make weight with a heavy-duty resealable plastic bag containing a salt brine solution comprised of 2 cups water and ½ ounce salt.
4. After you weigh the cabbage, cover the vessel's opening with a clean cloth towel or cheesecloth and secure it with a rubber band or string. If using an airlock, secure the airlock to your lid, fill the lock with water, and secure it to the top of the vessel. Place the vessel on the counter, out of the sunlight, where you can easily monitor it.
5. After a few days, begin tasting the cabbage, making sure to push the remaining cabbage down under the brine and remove any scum that might have formed on top. Once sauerkraut has a taste and texture you like, which may take up to 14 days, move ferment into the refrigerator to slow the fermentation process. Some prefer sauerkraut with a lightly fermented taste, whereas others prefer a stronger flavor.
6. Save sauerkraut juice as a brine for your next batch, or to drink as a healthy tonic. As you make more sauerkraut, keep notes on flavors and textures you like with days of fermentation tracked.

2. Scallion with Spiced Kimchi

Preparation Time: 10 minutes
Cooking Time: 0 minutes

INGREDIENTS:

- 2 lb (1 medium head) napa cabbage, roughly chopped
- 6 tbsp Diamond Crystal kosher salt, plus 1 to 2 tsp, if needed
- 4 cups water
- 1 bunch scallions
- 3 tbsp fine gochugaru
- 2 tbsp grated peeled fresh ginger
- 2 garlic cloves, pressed or minced

DIRECTION:

1. Place chopped cabbage in a large bowl or 1-gallon jar.
2. In a medium bowl, combine salt and water, stirring until salt dissolves. Pour brine over the cabbage and gently mix for a few minutes, ensuring all cabbage is covered. Cover the bowl and place it on the counter for 6 to 12 hours.
3. Drain the cabbage and squeeze out the brine, reserving ½ cup of brine. Taste cabbage; it should have a seawater–type saltiness. If it's too salty, lightly rinse it; if it's not salty enough, add 1 to 2 tsp salt to paste in step 4. Return the cabbage to its container. Add scallions.
4. In a small bowl, stir together 1 to 2 tsp salt (if needed, see step 3) gochugaru, ginger, and garlic, mixing well to create a paste. Add a small amount of brine if it seems dry. Rub the paste all over cabbage and scallions (you might want to wear gloves for this step, and avoid touching your face!), covering pieces as much as possible.
5. Pack cabbage tightly into a clean 1-gallon jar (you can use one you used in step 1, but wash it first) and remove any air bubbles. Put something on the cabbage to keep it submerged. If using a crock, use crock weights; if using a Mason jar, make weight with a heavy-duty resealable plastic bag containing a salt brine solution comprised of 2 cups water and ½ ounce salt.
6. After you weigh the cabbage, cover the vessel's opening with a clean cloth towel or cheesecloth and keep it with a rubber band or string. If using an airlock, secure the airlock to your jar lid, fill the lock with water, and keep it on top of the jar. Place the vessel on the counter away from sunlight.
7. After 4 days, start to taste kimchi, submerging cabbage in brine and removing any scum that might have formed over the top after every tasting. Once kimchi has your desired flavor, which may take up to 14 days, move the kimchi into the refrigerator to slow the fermentation process.

Notes:

3. Fermented Dill with Cucumber Pickles

Preparation Time: 10 minutes
Cooking Time: 25 minutes

INGREDIENTS:

- 2 lb (about 6) pickling cucumbers, stem end trimmed
- 2 fresh dill heads or 1 tbsp dried dill
- 1 head garlic, cloves separated and peeled
- 4 cups water
- 2 tbsp Diamond Crystal kosher salt

DIRECTION:

1. Examine cucumbers, making sure there are no soft, bruised, or discolored spots. Do a light wash and place cucumbers in a clean crock, glass jar, or glass jar with an airlock attachment. Add dill and garlic.
2. In a medium bowl, make the brine by combining water and salt, stirring until the salt dissolves. Pour brine over seasoned cucumbers. Put a weight on cucumbers to keep them submerged. If using a crock, use crock weights; if using a Mason jar, make weight with a heavy-duty resealable plastic bag containing a salt brine solution comprised of 2 cups water and ½ ounce salt.
3. After you weigh the pickles, cover the vessel's opening with a clean cloth towel or cheesecloth and tie it with a rubber band or string. If using an airlock, secure the airlock to your jar lid, fill the lock with water, and secure it to the top of the jar. Place the vessel on the counter in a cool, dry place.
4. Let cucumbers ferment for 2 weeks, removing any scum that forms on top. Depending on the temperature of your kitchen, cucumbers should be ready in about 2 weeks. The brine will be cloudy, and cucumbers will be translucent when cut open.
5. After this point, move the pickles into the refrigerator, where flavors will continue to develop over time.

Notes:

4. Garlicky Carrots with Celery

Preparation Time: 10 minutes
Cooking Time: 0 minutes

INGREDIENTS:

- 1 large head cauliflower, florets, and tender stem cut into small pieces (about 4 cups)
- 2 bell peppers, any color, thinly sliced
- 2 carrots, thinly sliced
- 2 celery stalks, diced
- 1 onion, thinly sliced
- 3 garlic cloves, thinly sliced
- 2 to 3 bay leaves
- 2 thyme sprigs or 2 tsp dried thyme
- 5 cups water
- 3 tbsp Diamond Crystal kosher salt

DIRECTION:

1. In a bowl, stir together cauliflower, bell peppers, carrots, celery, onion, and garlic. Put vegetables in the fermenting container and add bay leaves and thyme.
2. In a medium bowl, make the brine by combining water and salt, stirring until the salt dissolves. Pour brine over vegetables, packing vegetables down, so they are covered with brine.
3. Put a weight on vegetables to keep them submerged in the brine. If using a crock, use crock weights; if using a Mason jar, make weight with a heavy-duty resealable plastic bag containing a salt brine solution comprised of 2 cups water and ½ ounce salt.
4. After you weigh the mixture, cover the vessel's opening with a clean cloth towel or cheesecloth and tie it with a rubber band or string. If using an airlock, secure the airlock to your jar lid, fill the lock with water, and tie it to the top of the jar. Place the vessel on the counter, out of the sunlight.
5. Let the mixture ferment for 7 to 10 days, removing any scum that forms on top. When giardiniera has desired flavor, place it in the refrigerator to slow process, where it will keep for 3 to 6 months.

5. Fermented Chili Green Beans

Preparation Time: 10 minutes
Cooking Time: 0 minutes

INGREDIENTS:

- 1 to 1 ½ lb green beans, ends trimmed
- 2 garlic cloves, thinly sliced
- 4 chiles de Arbol or other small dried hot chili peppers
- 2 bay leaves
- 3 cups water
- 2 tbsp Diamond Crystal kosher salt

DIRECTION:

1. In a bowl, combine green beans and garlic. Transfer them to your fermenting container and add chili peppers and bay leaves.
2. In another medium bowl, make the brine by combining water and salt, stirring until the salt dissolves. Pour brine over vegetables, packing vegetables down, so they are covered with brine.
3. Put a weight on vegetables to keep them submerged in the brine. If using a crock, use crock weights; if using a Mason jar, make weight with a heavy-duty resealable plastic bag containing a salt brine solution comprised of 2 cups water and ½ ounce salt.
4. After you weigh green beans, cover the vessel's opening with a clean cloth towel or cheesecloth and tie it with a rubber band or string. If using an airlock, secure the airlock to your jar lid, fill the lock with water, and tie it to the top of the jar. Place the vessel on the counter, out of the sunlight.
5. Ferment for 1 week, removing any scum that forms on top. Once green beans have desired flavor (it may take a few more days), move them into the refrigerator to slow the process, where they will last for 3 to 6 months.

6. Vinegary Hot Sauce

Preparation Time: 10 minutes
Cooking Time: 0 minutes

INGREDIENTS:

- 2 cups sliced stemmed jalapeño peppers (include seeds and veins if you want a spicier sauce)
- 3 cups water
- 2 tbsp Diamond Crystal kosher salt
- 2 garlic cloves, peeled
- 1 cup distilled white vinegar or apple cider vinegar (optional)

DIRECTION:

1. Put jalapeños into a quart glass jar or container with enough room to accommodate brine and weight, if you are not using an airlock.
2. In a medium bowl, make the brine by combining water and salt, stirring until the salt dissolves. Pour brine over chiles, covering them by ½ inch. You may not need all brine. Tamp down chiles to remove any air pockets and make sure brine covers all jalapeño pieces.
3. Put a big thing on chiles to keep them submerged in the brine. If using a crock, use crock weights; if using a Mason jar, make weight with a heavy-duty resealable plastic bag containing a salt brine solution comprised of 2 cups water and ½ ounce salt.
4. After you weigh chiles, cover the vessel's opening with a clean cloth towel or cheesecloth and tie it with a rubber band or string. If using an airlock, secure the airlock to your jar lid, fill the lock with water, and tie it to the top of the jar. Place the vessel on the counter, away from sunlight.
5. Let chiles ferment for 3 to 4 weeks, removing any scum that forms on top. Chiles will be soft and a bit darker in color. If you taste a small piece, it will taste tangy and spicy. Tamp down chiles occasionally.
6. Once the fermenting time elapses, drain jalapeños, reserving brine.
7. In a blender, combine fermented jalapeños and garlic. Add either 1 cup of brine or 1 cup of vinegar (if you prefer flavor) and blend until smooth. If you want the hot sauce to be thinner, add more liquid.
8. Refrigerate, labeled, in an airtight glass jar for 2 to 3 months.

7. Vinegary Berry Shrub

Preparation Time: 10 minutes
Cooking Time: 20 minutes

INGREDIENTS:

- 3 cups fresh blackberries, washed and dried
- 1 ½ cups sugar
- 2 cups apple cider vinegar

DIRECTION:

1. In a large bowl, combine clean blackberries and sugar and smash them with your clean hands or a wooden spoon. Ensure the berries are completely smashed so you get adequate juice from berries. Pour the mixture into a large glass jar or container and add vinegar. Place a cover on the jar and shake it well.
2. Refrigerate the shrub for 1 week, shaking the jar when you remember. Taste the shrub each week to assess flavor development.
3. After 1 week, strain the mixture through a fine-mesh sieve to remove the seeds. You can use shrub at this point or reduce it on the stovetop to make flavors more concentrated.

8. Vinegary Red Wine

Preparation Time: 10 minutes
Cooking Time: 0 minutes

INGREDIENTS:

- 3 cups red wine (any type)
- ½ cup apple cider vinegar with "mother"

DIRECTION:

1. In a clean fermenting vessel, combine wine and vinegar. Cover the vessel's opening with a clean cloth towel or cheesecloth and secure it with a rubber band or string. If using an airlock, secure the airlock to your jar lid, fill the lock with water, tie it to the top of the jar and give the vessel a light shake. Place the vessel on the counter in a cool, dry place.
2. After 1 month, check the vinegar, removing any scum that forms on top. It should taste more like vinegar, and "mother" should be present.
3. Keep adding leftover wine to the vessel. If you add more than one-third amount of wine compared to vinegar, allow another month for vinegar to ferment. After 3 months, the vinegar will be ready.

9. Classic Milk Yogurt

Preparation Time: 10 minutes
Cooking Time: 10 minutes

INGREDIENTS:

- 3 cups whole milk
- 2 to 3 tbsp plain yogurt with live active cultures

DIRECTION:

1. In a pan over medium-high heat, heat the milk to 120°F, stirring gently. Use a thermometer to check the temperature.
2. Slowly stir together yogurt and ½ to 1 cup of warmed milk in a small bowl, mixing well. Return the milk-yogurt mixture to a saucepan of milk.
3. This mixture must maintain a temperature of between 115°F and 120°F during the period of fermentation. To get this, you have a few options: Place the mixture in an oven-safe container and into an oven with a strong pilot; place the mixture in an insulated cooler with hot water packs around the container; put the mixture into a multi cooker with a yogurt setting, or place mixture in a dehydrator set to 120°F.
4. Keep the yogurt mixture in this environment overnight or for 8 to 12 hours. Make sure the temperature doesn't drop (it will take yogurt longer to make) or become hotter (you might destroy microorganisms creating yogurt).
5. After 8 hours, check the yogurt to see if it has firmed up. If it is firm, move it to the refrigerator. If it has not firmed, let it ferment for 4 to 8 hours more, checking and tasting occasionally. The longer the fermentation time, the stronger, or more "sour," yogurt will become. When yogurt reaches a consistency and flavor you like, move it to the refrigerator. Don't forget to save some of your yogurts for your next batch. If you like Greek yogurt, strain yogurt in the refrigerator and overnight in a cheesecloth-lined sieve or colander placed over a bowl.

10. Sugared Kombucha with Fruit

Preparation Time: 10 minutes
Cooking Time: 0 minutes

INGREDIENTS:

- 16 cups water
- 4 black or green tea bags
- 1 ½ cups sugar
- 2 cups kombucha starter
- 1 SCOBY
- 1 to 2 cups pureed fruit (such as berries, melon, or tropical fruits) or fruit juice (try apple, cranberry, grape, or pineapple) (optional)

DIRECTION:

1. In a pot, bring water to a boil and add tea bags. Remove pot from heat. Stir in sugar, stirring until sugar dissolves, and let cool.
2. Once the tea is cool, remove and discard tea bags (strain tea through a fine-mesh sieve if using loose tea leaves).
3. Stir kombucha starter into tea. Empty tea into a glass jar or bottle and add SCOBY. Cover the vessel's top with a clean cloth towel or cheesecloth and secure it with a rubber band or string. Place the jar on the counter, away from heat and sunlight.
4. Let kombucha ferment for the next 7 to 10 days. Start to taste batch after 7 days. It should begin to taste sour. You will see a new layer of SCOBY starting to form.
5. Once kombucha has your desired taste, remove SCOBY. Place SCOBY and 1 to 2 cups of finished kombucha into a separate container to use as a starter for your next batch. Refrigerate it until ready to use.
6. Add pureed fruit or fruit juice to kombucha (if using) and pour it into a clean, reused soda bottle with a lock or screw top. Put a lid on the bottle and leave it on the counter for 1 to 3 days as it builds up carbonation. Check it each day to see how much pressure has built up. Move kombucha into the refrigerator to enjoy over the next 1 to 2 months.

Notes:

11. Fermented Caraway with Apple Salsa

Preparation Time: 10 minutes
Cooking Time: 0 minutes

INGREDIENTS:

- ½ cup filtered or non-chlorinated water
- 2 tbsp honey
- 2 tbsp whey (optional but useful; see sidebar elsewhere in this chapter for how to make whey)
- 2 cups apple
- 1 tbsp apple cider vinegar
- 2 tsp kosher or medium-grain sea salt
- 1 tsp coriander seeds
- ½ tsp caraway seeds
- ½ cup raisins
- ¼ cup thinly sliced onion
- 1 tsp ground cumin
- ½ to 1 tsp red pepper flakes
- ½ tsp dried thyme

DIRECTION:

1. Whisk water, honey, whey, apple cider vinegar, and salt until honey and salt are completely dissolved.
2. Peel and core apples. Chop them into pieces or slivers between ⅛ and ¼ inch thick.
3. Using a mortar and pestle, coarsely crush coriander and caraway seeds.
4. Chop raisins roughly (you can skip this step if you like, but I think the salsa texture is better if you take time).
5. Combine apples, raisins, onion pieces, and all of the spices in a sizable bowl. Organize combined ingredients in a quart-size, clean glass jar.
6. Add brine to other components. Add a little filtered water on top if the brine doesn't completely cover solid components.
7. Place a loose lid on the container (you want gases that develop during fermentation to be able to escape). A small plate should be placed beneath the jar to catch any spills that may happen during fermentation.
8. Leave the apple salsa jar out for two days at room temperature. At least once a day during that time, remove the cover to check for indications of fermentation, such as bubbles on the surface. If you lightly press on the meal, you'll particularly notice these. However, don't only keep an eye out for indications of fermentation; come near and use your nose to smell for that fresh-but-tangy pickled aroma that indicates the safe, delectable, and nutritious change you're wanting is taking place. Your fermenting fruit salsa will smell more aromatic than ordinary vegetable ferments because of the spices.
9. Move apple salsa to the refrigerator or a cold, dark cellar once it has been actively fermenting for at least 24 hours. Cool storage temperature will significantly slow down fermentation, so you won't need a plate underneath the jar anymore. This should prevent any overflow. If you decide to use the refrigerator, put apple salsa in the main compartment's top shelf, where it will stay the coolest. Apples

Notes:

12. Chili Miso with Pear Kimchi

Preparation Time: 10 minutes
Cooking Time: 0 minutes

INGREDIENTS:

- 4 tsp (20 mL) Ball® Salt for Pickling & Preserving, divided
- 2 cups (500 mL) water
- 4 unpeeled Asian pears (about 1 ¾ lb./875 g), quartered and cored
- 4 garlic cloves, peeled
- ½ cup (125 mL) Korean chili flakes
- ¼ cup (60 mL) water
- ¼ cup (60 mL) sugar
- 2 tbsp (30 mL) white miso
- 1 (1-inch/2.5-cm) piece fresh ginger, peeled and grated
- 2 bunches green onions, roots removed, green and white parts thinly sliced
- 2 (1-qt./1-L) canning jars
- 2 (4-oz/125-mL) Ball® jars

DIRECTION:

1. Combine 2 tsp (10 mL) salt and water in a 1-pt. (500-mL) jar, stirring until salt dissolves; cover with lid; set brine aside and reserve for later use.
2. Cut pear quarters crosswise into thin slices, and place in a bowl. Sprinkle pear slices with remaining 2 tsp (10 mL) salt; toss well. Close and let stand for 1 to 2 hours.
3. With the processor on, gradually drop garlic cloves through the food chute; process until minced. Add chili flakes and the next 4 ingredients. Process until paste forms, scraping sides as necessary. Stir paste and green onions into pear slices.
4. Divide the pear mixture evenly between 2 (1-qt./1-L) jars, pouring any remaining brine from the bottom of the bowl evenly over the pear mixture in both jars. (Jars will not be full, but brine should cover pear mixture by ½ inch (1 cm.) If the brine does not cover the pear mixture adequately, cover jars and let stand for 3 hours. If liquid still does not cover the pear mixture by ½ inch (1 cm), add reserved brine until the pear mixture is covered.
5. Fill 2 clean 4-oz (125-mL) Ball® jars with additional reserved brine, and set 1 jar on top of the pear mixture inside each 1-qt. (1-L) jar to weigh down the pear mixture. Place each jar in a cool (65°F to 75°F), dark place. Cover jars with a clean dish towel, and let stand for 24 hours.
6. After 24 hours, check to ensure the pear mixture remains submerged in the brine, and skim the white film from the top of the brine and around weights, if necessary. Taste kimchi, and if it has reached the desired flavor, remove weights. Wipe jars and refrigerate. If the kimchi has not reached the desired flavor, return weights to jars to keep the kimchi submerged. Cover and continue to let stand in a cool (65°F to 75°F), dark place for another day, or up to 1 week, until the desired flavor develops.
7. Once desired flavor is reached, remove weights; wipe jar rims, and cover jars with plastic lids. Store in refrigerator for up to 1 month.

Notes:

13. Gingered Cabbage Kimchi

Preparation Time: 10 minutes
Cooking Time: 0 minutes

INGREDIENTS:

- 2 tsp (10 mL), plus ¼ cup (60 mL), Ball® Salt for Pickling & Preserving
- 2 cups (500 mL) water
- 2 medium napa cabbages (about 2 lb./1 kg each)
- 6 garlic cloves, peeled
- 1 cup (250 mL) dried Korean chili flakes
- ⅓ cup (75 mL) grated fresh ginger
- 2 tbsp (30 mL) fish sauce
- 2 tbsp (30 mL) lite soy sauce
- 2 bunches green onions, root removed, green and white parts thinly sliced
- 2 to 3 unpeeled carrots, well-scrubbed and grated
- 2 (1-qt./1-L) canning jars
- 2 (4-oz/125-mL) canning jars

DIRECTION:

1. Combine 2 tsp (10mL) salt and water in a 1-pt. (500-mL) jar, stirring until salt dissolves; set brine aside and reserve for later use. Wash cabbage under cold running water. Reserve 2 cabbage leaves that are in good condition; set aside. Cut the remaining cabbage into quarters; core. Cut quarters into 2½-inch (6 cm)-wide ribbons. Place cabbage in a bowl and scatter with the remaining ¼ cup (60 mL) salt, massaging and squeezing salt into the cabbage until liquid is released. Cover the bowl, and let stand for 1 to 2 hours.
2. With the processor running, process garlic until minced. Add chili flakes and the next 3 ingredients. Process until paste forms; add to cabbage mixture. Add green onions and grated carrots to the cabbage mixture. Divide the cabbage mixture evenly between 2 (1-qt./1-L) jars, pressing down firmly with a wooden spoon and pouring any remaining brine from the bottom of the bowl evenly over the cabbage mixture in both jars. (Brine should cover cabbage mixture by ½-inch (1 cm.) If the brine does not cover the cabbage mixture adequately, cover jars, and let stand for 4 hours. If liquid still does not cover the cabbage mixture by ½ inch (1 cm), add reserved brine until the cabbage is covered.
3. Place 1 reserved cabbage leaf on top of the cabbage mixture in each jar, pushing down and tucking in the leaf to cover the mixture. Fill 2 clean 4-oz (125-mL) Ball® jars with water, and set 1 jar on top of cabbage mixture inside each 1-qt. (1-L) jar to weigh down the cabbage mixture. Place each jar on a plate i in a cool (65°F to 75°F), dark place. Close jars with a clean dish towel, and let them stand for 24 hours.
4. Check jars daily to ensure the cabbage mixture remains submerged in brine; skim the white film that forms. Return weights to jars to keep kimchi submerged; cover and continue to let stand in a cool (65°F to 75°F), dark place., checking daily.
5. After 4 days, check the flavor. If kimchi has reached the desired flavor, remove weights, wipe jar rims, and refrigerate. If the kimchi has not reached the desired flavor, return weights to jars to keep the kimchi submerged. Cover and continue to let stand in a cool (65°F to 75°F), dark place for another day or up to 2 weeks. Once desired flavor is reached, remove weights, wipe jar rims, and cover jars with lids. Store in refrigerator for up to 6 months.

Notes:

14. Fermented Ginger Bug

Preparation Time: 10 minutes
Cooking Time: 0 minutes

INGREDIENTS:

- ⅓ cup (75 mL) sugar, divided
- ⅓ cup (75 mL) grated unpeeled fresh organic ginger*, divided
- 1 (1-qt./1-L) canning jar
- 3 ½ cups (875 mL) non-chlorinated water or spring water**

DIRECTION:

1. Combine 2 tbsp (30 mL) of each sugar and ginger in a 1-qt. (1-L) canning jar. Add non-chlorinated water, stirring to dissolve sugar.
2. Close the jar with a clean cloth, and secure it with a rubber band or kitchen string. Let stand at room temperature for 3 days, adding 1 tsp (5 mL) of each sugar and grated ginger each day, stirring to dissolve sugar and replacing cloth after each addition.
3. On the fourth day, remove the cloth. Center lid on jar; apply band, and adjust loosely. Let stand for 4 more days or until mixture is very bubbly, adding sugar and ginger daily as above (warmer room temperature, sooner bubbles will form.)
4. Chill thoroughly. Keep in refrigerator and use within 2 weeks. Strain before using.

15. Cardamom with Worcestershire Sauce

Preparation Time: 10 minutes
Cooking Time: 0 minutes

INGREDIENTS:

- ¼ cup (60 mL) dark raisins
- ¼ cup (60 mL) boiling water
- ½ cup (125 mL) un-sulfured molasses
- ¼ cup (60 mL) jarred tamarind paste
- 1 (10-oz/284-g) onion, quartered
- 1 (½-inch/1-cm) piece peeled fresh ginger, chopped
- 1 garlic clove, crushed
- 2 cups (500 mL) white vinegar (5% acidity), divided
- 2 cardamom pods
- 2 tbsp (30 mL) Ball® Salt for Pickling & Preserving
- 2 tbsp (30 mL) dark brown sugar
- 1 tbsp (15 mL) dried crushed red pepper
- 1 tbsp (15 mL) dry mustard
- 1 tsp (5 mL) garlic powder
- 1 tsp (5 mL) whole cloves
- 1 tsp (5 mL) black peppercorns
- 1 tsp (5 mL) anchovy paste
- ½ tsp (2 mL) ground cinnamon
- 1 (1-qt./1-L) canning jar

DIRECTION:

1. Combine raisins and boiling water in a small bowl. Let stand 15 minutes or until the raisins are softened. Drain.
2. Process raisins, molasses, the next 4 ingredients, and 1 cup (250 mL) vinegar in a blender or food processor until smooth.
3. Remove seeds from cardamom pods; discard pods. Pour the raisin mixture into a medium saucepan; add cardamom seeds, salt, the next 8 ingredients, and the remaining 1 cup (250 mL) vinegar. Bring to a boil, stirring constantly. Remove from heat; cool.
4. Pour mixture into a 1-qt. (1-L) canning jar. Cover with a plastic lid. Store in a cool (65°F to 75°F), dark place for 2 to 4 weeks, depending upon desired strength, checking once a week.
5. Pour mixture through a fine wire-mesh sieve into a 1-qt. (1-L) glass measuring cup; discard solids. Pour into clean glass jars; cover with plastic lids. Store in refrigerator for 1 year.

16. Cinnamon with Fermented Pineapple Drink

Preparation Time: 10 minutes
Cooking Time: 0 minutes

INGREDIENTS:

- 1 cup (250 mL) sugar
- 1 (½-gal./2-L) canning jar
- 6 cups (1.5 L) of non-chlorinated water or spring water, divided
- 1 (3-inch/7.5-cm) cinnamon stick (optional)
- 2 whole cloves (optional)
- 1 very ripe pineapple
- Cheesecloth

DIRECTION:

1. Place sugar in a ½-gal. (2-L) jar. Add 1 qt. (1-L) non-chlorinated water, stirring until sugar dissolves. Add cinnamon and cloves, if desired.
2. Scrub pineapple; rinse with cold water. Using a sharp non-serrated knife, cut off a thin slice from the top and bottom of the pineapple, removing leaves and creating a flat surface on each end.
3. Position the pineapple upright on the cutting board. Thinly slice downward around the pineapple to remove rough skin, being careful not to waste fruit. Add skin to the sugar mixture in the jar.
4. Cut pineapple lengthwise into quarters. Cut the core away from each quarter; add pieces of the core to the jar, reserving fruit for another use. Add the remaining 2 cups (500 mL) water or until the jar is filled to within 1 inch (2.5 cm) of the top.
5. Close the jar with a clean cloth, and secure it with a rubber band or kitchen string. Let stand at room temperature for 12 to 24 hours or until the mixture is bubbly, scraping off any white foam that develops. If no bubbling at the top of the mixture occurs after 24 hours, center the lid on the jars. Apply bands, and adjust loosely. Let it stand for 12 more hours.
6. Empty mixture through a fine wire-mesh strainer lined with 3 layers of moist cheesecloth into a clean ½-gal. (2-L) jar or 2 (2-qt./2-L) jars. Center lids on jars. Apply bands, and adjust loosely. Chill thoroughly and store in the refrigerator for up to 2 weeks. Keep covered tightly to keep it bubbly.
7. To serve, pour over ice in tall glasses and dilute with the desired amount of water or mineral water.

Notes:

17. Mustardy Whole Grain

Preparation Time: 10 minutes
Cooking Time: 0 minutes

INGREDIENTS:

- 2 cups (500 mL) water
- 1 cup (250 mL) mustard seeds (a combination of brown and yellow seeds)
- 1½ tbsp (22 mL) salt
- ¼ cup (60 mL) dry mustard
- 2 tsp (10 mL) honey or sugar
- 1 ½ tsp (7.5 mL) sea salt
- ½ tsp (2 mL) garlic powder
- ¼ cup (60 mL) unfiltered apple cider vinegar (5% acidity)
- 1 tbsp (15 mL) fresh thyme leaves

DIRECTION:

1. Combine the first 3 ingredients in a bowl. Cover and let stand for 2 to 4 hours.
2. Drain mustard seeds in a wire-mesh strainer lined with a coffee filter or cheesecloth, discarding the liquid.
3. Pulse seeds in a food processor until crushed. Add dry mustard and the next 3 ingredients. Pulse until blended. Add vinegar; pulse just until blended.
4. Transfer the mustard mixture to a medium glass or nonmetallic bowl; stir in thyme. Cover with plastic wrap and let stand at room temperature for up to 3 days or until slightly bubbly, stirring daily.
5. Spoon mustard into clean ½-pt. (250-mL) jars. Remove air bubbles. Wipe jar rim. Center lid on jar. Apply the band, and adjust to fingertip-tight. Chill for 4 weeks before serving. Store in refrigerator for up to 1 year.

18. Loaded Sauerkraut

Preparation Time: 10 minutes
Fermentation Time: 2 to 6 weeks

INGREDIENTS:

- 1 ½ lb cabbage, shredded
- 1 onion, peeled, halved, and thinly sliced
- 6 garlic cloves, minced
- 2 medium turnips, peeled, halved, and thinly sliced
- 4 tsp pickling salt

DIRECTION:

1. In a large nonreactive bowl, mix all ingredients. Let mixture rest at room temperature for an hour to allow juices to begin loosening up cabbage and vegetables.
2. Pack cabbage and vegetables into a quart jar, using your fist to tamp them down as you go. Apply weight and close the jar using a nonreactive lid. Set the jar in a cool location.
3. After 1 day, check the sauerkraut to ensure that it is covered in its brine. If it isn't, add brine by mixing 1 cup of water with 1 tsp pickling salt and pouring over the sauerkraut until it is covered. Reapply the weight and place the jar in a cool location.
4. Check sauerkraut daily to ensure it remains submerged in its brine and that no scum appears. If scum appears on the surface, skim it off promptly, rinse the weight off, and reapply the weight. You will know fermentation has begun when tiny bubbles begin rising to the surface.
5. Ferment sauerkraut for 2 to 6 weeks. After 2 weeks, begin tasting sauerkraut. If it is soured to your liking, place it in the refrigerator at this time. If not, continue with fermentation until you are satisfied with the flavor.
6. Once fermentation is complete, transfer the sauerkraut to the refrigerator. It can be eaten immediately, but it will continue to cure for the next month and the flavor will develop further. Refrigerated, sauerkraut will last for several months.

19. Kale Kraut

Preparation Time: 10 minutes
Fermentation time: 2 to 6 days

INGREDIENTS:

- 15 cups tightly packed kale leaves
- 2 garlic cloves, minced
- 1 tbsp pickling salt
- 2 lemon wedges

DIRECTION:

1. Prepare the kale by stacking several leaves at a time, rolling them up, and then thinly slicing them into strips. As you work, transfer kale to a large bowl. If you are using baby kale, you can choose whether to shred kale or leave the leaves whole.
2. Add garlic and salt to the bowl and mix thoroughly.
3. Pack kale into a quart jar, tucking lemon wedges into the top. Close the jar with a nonreactive lid and leave it at room temperature for 2 to 4 days. Transfer kale to the refrigerator, where its flavors will mellow over 3 to 5 days. Refrigerated, this kraut will keep for 2 weeks.

20. Lacto-Fermented Ginger Carrots

Preparation Time: 10 minutes
Fermentation Time: 7 to 14 days

INGREDIENTS:

- 1 (2-inch) piece of ginger, peeled and cut into matchsticks
- 1 lb carrots, peeled and cut into sticks about 4 to 6 inches long
- 1 tbsp plus 1 tsp pickling salt
- 3 cups water

DIRECTION:

1. Pack ginger into the jar and add carrots, packing them in snugly. In a measuring cup, mix salt and water until the salt is dissolved, and pour the brine over the carrots. Use a weight to keep carrots submerged in the brine. Cover the jar using a nonreactive lid and leave the jar at room temperature.
2. Carrots will be ready in 7 to 14 days. Test them at around 7 days by removing a stick with a clean utensil and cutting off a small piece for a taste before returning it. If it tastes good, they are done. If they're not yet to your liking, reapply weight to carrots and continue fermentation for up to another week.
3. When fermentation is complete, remove the weight and cap the jar with a nonreactive lid. Transfer the jar to the refrigerator, where carrots will keep for at least 2 weeks.

Notes:

21. Lacto-Fermented Asparagus

Preparation Time: 10 minutes
Fermentation Time: 7 to 14 days

INGREDIENTS:

- 1 lb asparagus, trimmed to at least 1 inch shorter than the jar
- 6 garlic cloves, crushed
- 1 tsp black peppercorns
- ½ tsp mixed pickling spice
- ½ cup fermented vegetable brine
- 1 ½ cups water
- 1 tbsp pickling salt

DIRECTION:

1. Wash and dry asparagus. Pack garlic, peppercorns, and mixed pickling spice into the jar. Fit asparagus snugly in the jar, tips all either up or down, leaving about 1 inch of headspace.
2. Pour vegetable brine over the asparagus. In a small bowl, mix water and salt until salt is dissolved. Pour this over the asparagus to cover it. If it is not covered, add a little more water until it is. If necessary, add a weight to hold the asparagus submerged in the brine. Cover the jar with a nonreactive lid and leave the jar in a room-temperature location.
3. After a day or two, bubbles should begin to form and rise in the jar, signaling fermentation. Watch the jar every day, and if any scum appears on the brine's surface, skim it off and rinse weight. Repack the weight into the mouth of the jar and continue fermentation.
4. Test asparagus after 10 days by removing a piece with a clean utensil and cutting off a small slice for a taste before returning it. If it tastes good, it's done. If they're not yet to your liking, return the weight to the mouth of the jar and continue fermentation for up to 14 days total.
5. When fermentation is complete, remove weight, cap jar with a nonreactivc lid, and transfer it to the refrigerator, where spears will keep for about 1 month.

22. Lacto-Fermented Radishes

Preparation Time: 10 minutes
Fermentation Time: 7 to 14 days

INGREDIENTS:

- 1 ½ lb radishes, sliced
- 2 cups water
- 1 ½ tbsp pickling salt

DIRECTION:

1. Pack radishes into a quart jar. Mix water and salt together, stirring until salt dissolves. Pour brine over radishes. Weight radishes with a jelly jar or other weight to submerge all of the radishes in brine. Leave the jar at room temperature.
2. After 5 days, check the radishes for taste. If they taste good, they are done. If you're not satisfied yet with their flavor, reapply weight and return them to the counter to ferment for up to 10 days total.
3. When fermentation is complete, remove weight, cap jar with a nonreactive lid, and transfer it to the refrigerator, where radishes will keep for about 1 month.

23. Lacto-Fermented Beans

Preparation Time: 10 minutes
Fermentation Time: 7 to 14 days

INGREDIENTS:

- ½ lb green beans
- 2 dill heads
- 4 garlic cloves, crushed
- ½ tsp black peppercorns, crushed
- 3 cups water
- 2 tbsp pickling salt

DIRECTION:

1. Layer beans, dill, garlic, and peppercorns in a quart jar. Mix together water and salt in a small bowl, stirring until the salt is dissolved. Pour brine over beans, using a weight to hold beans below the brine, if needed.
2. After 7 days, check beans for taste. If they are to your liking, they are done. If you're not yet satisfied with their flavor, reapply weight and return them to the counter to ferment for up to 14 days total.
3. When fermentation is complete, remove weight, cap jar with a nonreactive lid, and transfer it to the refrigerator, where beans will keep for about 1 month.

24. Mixed Garden Pickles

Preparation Time: 10 minutes
Fermentation Time: 7 to 14 days

INGREDIENTS:

- 1 to 2 cauliflower heads, separated into florets
- 1 bell pepper, cut into strips
- ½ lb green beans
- 1 onion, peeled and sliced
- 1 cup carrots, peeled and cut into ½-inch rounds
- 4 garlic cloves, crushed
- 1 thyme sprig
- ½ tsp crushed black peppercorns
- 4 tbsp pickling salt
- 6 cups water
- 1 tbsp red wine vinegar

DIRECTION:

1. In a bowl, toss all vegetables together. Pack vegetables into a jar and add garlic, thyme, and peppercorns. Process brine by dissolving salt in water and pouring it over vegetables. Add vinegar.
2. Weigh vegetables down below the brine using a small weight inserted into the mouth of the jar, or use a zip-top bag filled with remaining brine and insert this into the mouth of the jar. Leave the jar at room temperature.
3. Fermentation should be noticeable after 3 to 5 days, as bubbles will form in the jar. Check the jar daily, and immediately skim off the scum that appears on the surface, clean the weight, and add it back to the jar.
4. Check pickles for doneness after about 2 weeks. If they are soured to your liking, they are ready. If not, add weight back to the jar and continue to ferment for 3 weeks total. When fermentation is complete, remove weight, cover with a nonreactive lid, and refrigerate. These pickles will keep for over 1 month.

25. Dilly Mixed Garden Pickles

Preparation Time: 10 minutes
Fermentation Time: 7 to 14 days

INGREDIENTS:

- 2 cups whole small sweet peppers
- 2 cups pickling cucumbers, cut into 1-inch rounds
- 2 cups carrots, peeled and cut into 1-inch rounds
- 2 cups thinly sliced cabbage
- 1 cup green beans, cut in half
- 4 garlic cloves, crushed
- 2 dill heads
- ½ tsp crushed black peppercorns
- ½ tsp red chili pepper flakes
- 1 lemon, sliced
- 1 ½ tbsp pickling salt
- 2 cups water
- ¼ cup white vinegar

DIRECTION:

1. In a large bowl, toss all vegetables together. Pack vegetables into a jar, layering in garlic, dill, peppercorns, chili flakes, and lemon. Process brine by dissolving salt in water and pouring it over vegetables. Add vinegar.
2. Weigh vegetables down below the brine using a small weight inserted into the mouth of the jar, or use a zip-top bag filled with remaining brine, and insert this into the mouth of the jar. Leave the jar at room temperature.
3. Fermentation should be noticeable after 3 to 5 days, as bubbles will form in the jar. Check the jar daily, and immediately skim off the scum that appears on the surface, clean the weight, and add it back to the jar.
4. Check pickles for doneness after about 1 week. If they are soured to your liking, they are ready. If not, add weight back to the jar and continue to ferment for 3 weeks total. When fermentation is complete, remove weight, cover with a nonreactive lid, and refrigerate. These pickles will keep for several months.

26. Lacto-Fermented Turnips and Beets

Preparation Time: 10 minutes
Fermentation Time: 7 to 14 days

INGREDIENTS:

- 2 lb turnips, peeled and shredded
- ½ lb beets, peeled and shredded
- 1 ½ tbsp pickling salt

PAIR WITH: Pickled turnips make a great addition of flavor and color to a green salad. Serve a generous portion, along with carrots, lettuce, scallions, slivered almonds, and feta cheese, and you have a delicious and filling meal.

DIRECTION:

1. In a large bowl, toss turnips and beets. Add salt and mix well. Pack turnips and beets into a quart jar. Add weight to the turnip-beet mixture by inserting a jelly jar or other weight into the mouth of the jar. Place a nonreactive lid loosely on the jar, and set the jar in a location between 60°F and 75°F.
2. The following day, check to see that the turnip-beet mixture is submerged in the brine. If not, mix 2 ½ tsp pickling salt with 2 cups of water and add to the jar. Reapply the weight and lid and return the jar to its location.
3. Check ferment daily for scum on its surface; if it does appear, skim it off and rinse weights before adding them back to the jar.
4. After 2 weeks, check turnips for taste. If they are to your liking, they are done. If you are not yet satisfied, reapply the weight and return them to the counter to ferment for up to 6 weeks total, checking for doneness every couple of days.
5. When fermentation is complete, remove weight, cap the jar with a nonreactive lid, and transfer it to the refrigerator, where turnips will keep for more than 1 month.

27. Lacto-Fermented Daikon

Preparation Time: 10 minutes
Fermentation Time: 7 days

INGREDIENTS:

- 1 lb daikon
- 4 dried chili peppers
- 1 (2-inch) piece of ginger, peeled and sliced
- 2 cups water
- 1 ½ tbsp pickling salt

DIRECTION:

1. Cut the daikon in half lengthwise and then slice each half into ½-inch-thick half-moons. Layer daikon in a quart jar along with chili peppers and ginger. Combine water and salt, stir until the salt is dissolved completely, and pour the brine over the daikon until it is covered. Weigh daikon down with a small weight inserted into the mouth of the jar. Cap the jar loosely with a nonreactive lid, and leave the jar at room temperature to ferment.
2. Daikon will be complete after 2 to 3 days. When you are satisfied with the sourness of the pickle, remove weight, cap the jar with a nonreactive lid, and transfer it to the refrigerator, where the daikon will keep for about 1 month.

28. Lacto-Fermented Eggplant

Preparation Time: 10 minutes
Fermentation Time: 7 to 14 days

INGREDIENTS:

- 4 small Japanese or other Asian-variety eggplants
- 10 garlic cloves, crushed
- ½ tsp crushed black peppercorns
- ½ tsp red chili pepper flakes
- 1 tsp dried oregano
- 2 tbsp pickling salt
- 3 cups water

DIRECTION:

1. Peel eggplants and then thinly slice them. Pack them into a pint jar, layering them with garlic, peppercorns, chili pepper flakes, and oregano. In a small bowl, mix salt and water, stirring until the salt is dissolved. Pour brine over eggplant. Use a small weight to hold the eggplant down under the brine. Loosely cap the jar with a nonreactive lid and leave the jar in a room-temperature location.
2. After 7 days, remove weight, cap jar with a nonreactive lid, and transfer it to the refrigerator, where eggplant will keep for at least 1 month.

Notes:

Fruits and Vegetables

29. Raw Fermented Beets

Preparation Time: 1 week
Cooking Time: 0 minutes

INGREDIENTS:

- 2 lb beets, peeled & cut into chunks
- 4 cloves gochugaru garlic, peeled
- 6 peppercorns
- 2 bay leaves

Brine:

- 3 cups water, boiled and cooled
- 1 tbsp salt

DIRECTION:

1. Divide chunks of beet in between 2 jars with lids. Place 1 bay leaf, 2 cloves garlic, and 3 peppercorns into each jar.
2. In a bowl, mix salt and water to make the brine and stir until the salt is dissolved completely. Add enough brine into jars to cover the beets completely.
3. Close with lids and allow jars to stand at room temperature for about 1 week until foam begins to appear at the top. Place jars in a cool place (10°C, 50°F) for 2 to 3 days once foam appears. Keep in fridge.

30. Fermented Onions

Preparation Time: 1 hour + 3-4 weeks fermenting time
Cooking Time: 0 minutes

INGREDIENTS:

- 3 cups onions, peeled
- 2 tbsp salt
- 4 cups water

DIRECTION:

1. Prepare onions and add them to the jar, leaving 1-inch headspace.
2. Combine salt and water and pour into a jar.
3. Seal the jar with a lid and store it in a dark place. Open once a day to release gas before sealing again.
4. Repeat for 3 to 4 weeks until there are no more bubbles. Store in fridge.

31. Bok Choy White Kimchi

Preparation Time: 3 hours + 1-2 weeks fermenting time
Cooking Time: 0 minutes

INGREDIENTS:

- 1 Korean radish
- 3 tbsp salt
- 1 kg bok choy
- ½ ripe and cored pear
- ½ white onion
- 2 garlic cloves
- 1 fresh ginger piece
- 3 green chilies
- ½ tsp fish sauce
- 3 green onions
- ½ bunch of cilantros

DIRECTION:

1. Start by slicing or shredding radish. Cut bok choy into quarters. Add these cutdown radishes and bok choy to a large bowl.
2. Take 3 tbsp salt and add to radish and bok choy. Cover the bowl and let it be for one to 3 hours at room temperature.
3. Take a good-quality chopper. Add chilies, garlic, ginger, onions, puree of pear, and fish sauce only if you want, and start the blender. Make a smooth paste of all these ingredients.
4. After the required time, wash Korean radish and bok choy with water and rinse them thoroughly. Now strain and squeeze them to take out water. Ensure that there is no water in the bok choy.
5. Chop green onions and cilantro to add them to the veggies. Now add the paste to this mixture.
6. Take jars and fill them with these spiced radishes and bok choy. Shake the jar and stir it so that there is no air left inside.
7. Make sure the seal is tight but slightly loosened on ⅛ turn. Store these jars for 2 weeks in dark. Maintain room temperature and when these veggies are pickled according to your requirement, store them in the fridge. You can store them for up to a year.

32. Fermented Lemons

Preparation Time: 14 minutes + 2 weeks fermenting time
Cooking Time: 0 minutes

INGREDIENTS:

- 5 to 6 lemons
- 3 tbsp sea salt

DIRECTION:

1. Clean lemons and cut them into pieces, either in slices or quarters, as preferred.
2. Sprinkle salt on the lemon and put it into the jar. When full, squish, add more salt and juice, and combine into the brine.
3. Only stop when lemons aren't totally submerged in juice, and the jar is completely full. Then, juice another lemon or two on top.
4. Sprinkle a bit more salt, then put plastic wrap over and push the lemons down. You want them all submerged in juice.
5. Throw the lid on and let sit in the open for 2 weeks. Turn over the jar each day to keep salt from settling.
   After two weeks, put it back into the fridge.

33. Tomato Ketchup

Preparation Time: 10 minutes + 2 to 3 days fermenting time
Cooking Time: 0 minutes

INGREDIENTS:

- 6 oz tomato paste
- 1 tbsp honey or maple syrup
- 2 tbsp starter liquid (whey, sauerkraut juice, or water kefir)
- ¼ tsp salt
- 1 garlic clove
- ⅛ tsp cinnamon powder
- 1 pinch cayenne
- 1 pinch of ground cloves
- 2 tbsp apple cider vinegar

DIRECTION:

1. Take a ready-made tomato paste or make it yourself by blending tomatoes.
2. Now, take this paste in a bowl and add starter liquid to it. Mix it well and add salt, cinnamon, garlic, honey, cloves, and cayenne. Mix them thoroughly to make a homogeneous paste.
3. Now, transfer this paste to the jar and shake it well.
4. Take apple cider vinegar and pour it over the ketchup surface. This addition of vinegar prevents the growth of microbes on the surface.
5. Now, you have to store it in a jar at room temperature. Ensure maintenance of temperature and no entry of light. Keep them in the same conditions for 3 days.
6. When ketchup is fermented to the required state, stir the whole mixture to mix vinegar with the rest of the ketchup. You can keep it in your fridge for 2 to 3 weeks.
7. The consistency of ketchup depends on the quantity of starter liquid. If you add enough starter liquid, the ketchup will become thinner.

34. Sauerkraut (Simple Cultured Cabbage)

Preparation Time: 20 minutes + 3 days- 2 weeks fermenting time
Cooking Time: 0 minutes

INGREDIENTS:

- 1 to 2 tbsp mineral salt
- 1 to 2 heads of cabbage, 2 lb

DIRECTION:

1. With a mandolin, shred the cabbage.
2. Add salt (2 tsp) to the cabbage and massage it. Add more salt (but not too much) to make it salty.
3. Let it rest for half an hour. Add to a jar, and push down with clean hands.
4. Leave a 3-inch space from above. Add 2 to 3 cabbage leaves
5. Check it every day, and taste it after 3rd day. Let it ferment for 3 days to 2 weeks based on your desired flavor profile.
6. Store in fridge with a lid.

Notes:

Dairy and Bread

35. Homemade Greek Yogurt

Preparation Time: 50 minutes
Cooking Time: 0 minutes

INGREDIENTS:

- 1 quart (32 oz) homemade yogurt

DIRECTION:

1. Fold a large piece of cheesecloth over itself (doubling its thickness) and lay it on top of a large bowl.
2. Pour yogurt on your cheesecloth.
3. Take all of the edges of your cheesecloth, then bring them together to have a yogurt bundle. Use a rubber band to seal the cheesecloth around the yogurt wholly.
4. After securing your bundle, use one or two more rubber bands to hang it from a shelf or cabinet over the mixing bowl so that gravity helps drain whey (liquid) from yogurt.
5. Allow yogurt to strain for 45 minutes to an hour.
6. Release the yogurt bundle from its rubber band hold and open up the cheesecloth. Yogurt should look thick and kind of stringy.

Notes:

36. Cultured Buttermilk

Preparation Time: 24 to 36 hours
Cooking Time: 0 minutes

INGREDIENTS:

- 1 cup active cultured buttermilk
- 4 cups whole milk

DIRECTION:

1. Purchase a container of active cultured buttermilk. This shouldn't be too hard to find. Most grocery stores carry active cultured buttermilk. Try to find a new container that hasn't been sitting on the shelf for a long time. The closer buttermilk is to its expiration date, the fewer active cultures it will have.
2. Add 1 cup of active cultured buttermilk to 4 cups of whole milk. Stir buttermilk into whole milk and pour the mixture into a glass jar.
3. Place the lid tightly on the jar and let the jar sit at room temperature for 24 hours. Check buttermilk to see if it has clabbered. If not, let it sit for another 12 hours. If it hasn't clabbered by this point, throw out the batch and try again with new buttermilk.
4. Move finished buttermilk to the fridge.
5. Once you've made a batch of buttermilk, you can use a cup of buttermilk from your old batch to make the next batch as long as it isn't too old. As long as you stay on top of things, you can continue making new batches using buttermilk from earlier batches indefinitely.

37. Sourdough Bread

Preparation Time: 3 hours + 12 to 24 hours processing time
Cooking Time: 0 minutes

INGREDIENTS:

- ½ cup sourdough starter
- 1 ¼ bottled water
- 3 ¼ cups all-purpose flour
- 2 tbsp spices and whole seeds
- 1 tsp salt

DIRECTION:

1. Take a large bowl for mixing and add a sourdough starter. Now, pour all of the water into the sourdough.
2. Add all-purpose flour or whole-grain flour, according to your choice, to the bowl. Mix all of the ingredients already put in the bowl. Keep mixing and kneading sourdough until it absorbs all water. The dough will be shaggy, cover it using a towel and leave it to rest for 20 minutes.
3. Now add salt to the surface of the sourdough by sprinkling equally. Knead this dough well for 5 to 10 minutes. The dough will not be shaggy anymore but will be consistent.
4. Leave sourdough covered with a towel for 1 ½ hour. Check the dough every 30 minutes and keep folding it from its corners.
5. You should not disturb this covered dough for another 6 to 7 hours. It will double itself during this time.
6. When 6 hours have passed, uncover the dough, fold it and make a ball, and leave it to rest for almost 20 minutes.
7. After 20 minutes, tightly shape the dough, and transfer it to an olive oil-coated bowl. Leave it undisturbed and covered for another one to 2 hours.
8. Meanwhile, ready your oven by preheating it at 475°F. Score the top of the dough using a bread knife and let it get baked for 10 minutes. After 10 minutes, lower oven temperature to 400°F. Now, bake the dough for 25 minutes more. After 25 minutes, turn off the oven and transfer the dough to a cooling rack. Wait for it to cool down before slicing it.

38. Queso Fresco

Preparation Time: 2 hours + 6 hours processing time
Cooking Time: 0 minutes

INGREDIENTS:

- 1 gallon of milk
- 1 packet of mesophilic starter
- 2 tbsp salt
- ⅛ tsp rennet diluted with ¼ cup water
- Cheese mold

DIRECTION:

1. Pour one gallon of milk into a large pot and put it on the stove. Keep flame high, then wait till milk temperature reaches 90°F.
2. Remove the pot when it reaches this temperature. Add starter to milk while continuously stirring the milk. Leave this mixture for 40 minutes. Make sure to cover the pot while waiting.
3. Add ⅛ tsp rennet to ¼ cup of water. Stir water and rennet to combine them. Then cover this mixture and let it be for 45 minutes. Check for visible curd after 45 minutes have passed. This layer will be right below the whey layer. Check curd using a butter knife. The mixture is ready if pressing with a knife makes the butter break at the surface.
4. Wait for the cheese to set into a mass. Then cut this semi-solid cheese into cubes no longer than ¼ inch. Cover cheese for 5 minutes.
5. Put the pot on the stove to cook the curd. Maintain temperature at 90°F and keep stirring curd unless the whey layer separates from it completely.
6. Strain curd using a sieve and make cheese from this curd using a cheese mold. Press curd with appropriate weight and add salt to the cheese. Keep cheese undisturbed for 4 to 5 hours.
7. When 4 hours have passed, check the cheese. If you are satisfied with the texture, keep it in the fridge for 2 weeks at best.

39. Fermented Kefir

Preparation Time: 20 minutes + 2 to 4 days processing time
Cooking Time: 0 minutes

INGREDIENTS:

- 1 oz kefir grains
- 7 oz milk

DIRECTION:

1. In a glass jar (1 pint), add kefir & milk.
2. Close with a paper towel and place a rubber band around the paper towel.
3. Keep in a darker environment or cool environment for 12 to 48 hours, and strain after 12, 48 hours to get your desired taste.
4. Do not wash jars in between straining; replace jar after 4 days.

Notes:

Beverages

40. Batch-Brewed Kombucha Tea

Preparation Time: 15 minutes + 7 days processing time
Cooking Time: 5 minutes

INGREDIENTS:

- 4 bags of your favorite green or black tea
- 1 cup organic cane sugar
- ¼ cup vinegar
- 8 cups filtered water

DIRECTION:

1. Wash your hands with apple cider vinegar. Don't use antibacterial hand wash or soap because it can interfere with bacteria in kombucha.
2. Place water in a pot over high heat. Bring water to a boil and let it boil for at least 5 minutes. Turn off the heat and immediately place tea bags in water. Add sugar to water and stir it in.
3. Wait for the tea to cool to room temperature, and pour the tea into a glass jar. Add vinegar to tea. If you have access to kombucha tea that hasn't been pasteurized or otherwise processed, you can use a cup of tea instead. Vinegar (or tea) is necessary to get the pH of tea low enough to prevent bad bacteria or mold from developing.
4. Add kombucha starter culture to tea. Avoid directly touching it if at all possible. Cover the top of the jar with cheesecloth or cloth and band it or tie it down.
5. Place the jar somewhere dark and warm. The ideal temperature range is 80°F to 87°F. Avoid fermenting kombucha at temperatures below 70°F because bad bacteria, mold, and pathogens are more likely to form.
6. Let tea ferment for 7 days. SCOBY culture may float to the top during the fermentation process. This is fine. Baby SCOBY will typically form at the surface of kombucha, eventually forming a new SCOBY that acts as a protective barrier. Dip a straw into the tea and block the straw off with your finger to trap the tea inside. You can either taste tea to see if it tastes like vinegar or check pH to see if it's around 3. More brewing time is needed if it tastes too sweet or the pH is above 3.
7. Remove the mother culture and any smaller SCOBY cultures that may have formed and place them in a clean non-reactive container. Cover them with kombucha to keep them safe.
8. Move finished kombucha tea to glass containers and place a lid on them. If you're happy with the carbonation level of kombucha, loosely cap containers. On the other hand, if you want more carbonation, tightly cap containers. Let kombucha ferment for another 3 to 5 days before either drinking it or moving it to the fridge to slow the fermentation process.
9. Periodically open container to allow gases trapped inside to escape.

41. Ginger Kombucha

Preparation Time: 15 minutes + 7 days processing time
Cooking Time: 5 minutes

INGREDIENTS:

- 4 bags of your favorite green or black tea
- 1 cup organic cane sugar
- 1 cup homemade kombucha tea
- 8 cups filtered water
- 3 to 4 ginger slices

DIRECTION:

1. Wash your hands with vinegar. Place water in a pot on the stove and bring it to a boil. Add tea bags, then turn off the stove. Once the water stops boiling, add cane sugar and stir it in. Let the tea cool to room temperature.
2. Remove tea bags, then place sweet tea in a glass fermenting container. Add a cup of kombucha tea and place SCOBY in the container with the tea. Cover the container loosely with a piece of cloth and band it so that it won't come off.
3. Let tea ferment for 7 days. Remove SCOBY culture and prepare it for safekeeping or move it to another batch of kombucha. Place kombucha in bottles with ginger slices and cap bottles tightly. Let bottles sit for another 4 to 5 days. Open the bottle at least once a day to let gases out, or you run the risk of exploding bottles.
4. Once carbonation has developed to your liking, move bottles to the fridge to slow the fermentation process.

42. Cherry Lime Soda

Preparation Time: 15 minutes + 2 to 3 days processing time
Cooking Time: 0 minutes

INGREDIENTS:

- 2 cups 100% cherry juice
- 5 limes, juiced
- 8 cups water kefir

DIRECTION:

1. Add all ingredients to your pitcher or jug and stir together. Pour into sealable bottles and seal.
2. Leave bottles at room temperature for 2 to 3 days before consuming or placing them in the refrigerator

43. Cabbage and Carrot Fermented Juice

Preparation Time: 15 minutes + 4 to 6 days processing time
Cooking Time: 0 minutes

INGREDIENTS:

- ½ head cabbage, sliced
- 3 carrots, grated
- 1 tbsp ginger, grated
- 2 tsp sea salt
- Bottled spring water for soaking vegetables
- 2-quart jar
- Cheesecloth or kitchen towel
- Rubber band
- Long handle spoon for stirring

DIRECTION:

1. Place cabbage, carrots, ginger, and sea salt in a 2-quart jar.
2. Fill the jar with spring or well water.
3. Place cheesecloth or a kitchen towel over the jar and secure it with a rubber band to keep bugs out.
4. For four to six days, leave the jar in a warm, dark place. If bubbles and grayish foam form on the surface of the liquid, it is quite normal, stir well twice a day. When the juice is finished, it will smell sour, yeasty, and vinegary (not rotten).
5. Strain juice off vegetables and either drink immediately or pour into a sealable jar or bottle and keep in the refrigerator for up to one week.

PICKLING RECIPES

Vegetables

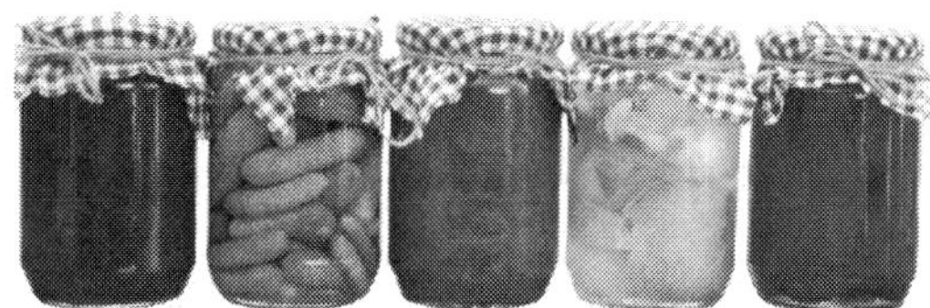

44. Pickled Cherry Tomatoes

Preparation Time: 10 minutes
Cooking Time: 10 minutes

INGREDIENTS:

- 4 cups cherry tomatoes
- 2 cups water
- 1 cup vinegar
- 2 sprigs of fresh rosemary
- 2 garlic cloves
- ½ tsp salt

DIRECTION:

1. Add vinegar, water, and salt to a saucepan and boil over medium heat. Turn heat to low, then simmer for 10 minutes.
2. Pack cherry tomatoes in clean jars.
3. Add garlic cloves and rosemary on top of the tomatoes.
4. Pour hot brine over tomatoes. Leave ¼-inch headspace.
5. Seal jar with lids. Process in your water bath canner for 10 minutes.
6. Remove jars from the water bath and let them cool completely.
7. Check the seals of jars. Label and store.

45. Garlic Pickles

Preparation Time: 10 minutes
Cooking Time: 20 minutes

INGREDIENTS:

- 12 garlic heads (separated into cloves, peeled)
- 1 tbsp pickling salt
- 2 ½ cups white vinegar
- 1 tbsp dried oregano
- 1 cup white wine
- 5 dried red chili peppers
- 1 tbsp sugar

DIRECTION:

1. Clean jars and put chile pepper in each one.
2. In a saucepan, combine wine, vinegar, oregano, salt, and sugar and bring to a gentle boil for a minute.
3. Remove your pan from heat and add garlic.
4. Fill sterilized jars halfway with mixture, allowing a half-inch headspace.
5. Clean rims and remove any air bubbles.
6. Place lids on jars, then attach bands, ensuring sure they are tight.
7. Process jars for 10 minutes in a hot water canner that has been prepared.
8. Remove jars from the oven, set them aside to cool, and then label them.

46. Pickled Carrots

Preparation Time: 10 minutes
Cooking Time: 10 minutes

INGREDIENTS:

- 1 lb carrots, peeled and sliced into sticks
- 1 tbsp sugar
- $^1/_3$ cup water
- $^2/_3$ cup of apple cider vinegar
- ½ tsp sea salt

DIRECTION:

1. Pack sliced carrot sticks into the clean jar.
2. Add water, vinegar, sugar, and salt into a small saucepan and cook over medium heat until the sugar is dissolved.
3. Pour hot brine over carrots in a jar.
4. Seal the jar with a lid and store it in the refrigerator.

47. Pickled Cucumbers

Preparation Time: 10 minutes
Cooking Time: 60 minutes

INGREDIENTS:

- 1 cucumber, thinly sliced
- ½ cup water
- ½ cup apple cider vinegar
- 1 tbsp sugar
- 1 ½ tsp kosher salt

DIRECTION:

1. Mix water, vinegar, sugar, and salt in your medium bowl. Stir until sugar is dissolved.
2. Add sliced cucumbers into a bowl and let soak for 1 hour.
3. Pour pickled cucumbers into a clean jar and seal the jar with a lid.
4. Once a jar is open, then store it in the refrigerator.

48. Pickled Jalapeno

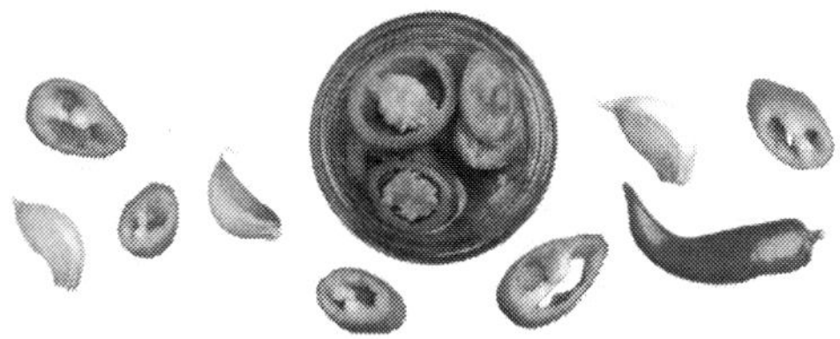

Preparation Time: 10 minutes
Cooking Time: 15 minutes
Servings: 2

INGREDIENTS:

- 10 jalapeno peppers, sliced into rings
- ½ tsp oregano
- 1 garlic clove, crushed
- 3 tbsp white sugar
- ¾ cup vinegar
- ¾ cup water
- 1 tbsp kosher salt

DIRECTION:

1. Add water, oregano, garlic, sugar, vinegar, and salt into a saucepan and bring to a boil over high heat.
2. Stir in jalapeno peppers. Remove the pan from heat, then let it cool for 10 minutes.
3. Pour pickled jalapeno with brine into a clean jar. Seal the jar with a lid, then store it in the refrigerator.

49. Pickled Radishes

Preparation Time: 10 minutes
Cooking Time: 10 minutes
Servings: 6

INGREDIENTS:

- ½ lb radishes, remove stem & root & cut into $1/8$-inch slices
- 1 bay leaf
- ½ tsp ground black pepper
- 1 tsp mustard seeds
- ¼ cup water
- ½ cup sugar
- ½ cup apple cider vinegar
- 1 tsp salt

DIRECTION:

1. Add sliced radishes into the clean jar.
2. Add vinegar, sugar, water, mustard seeds, black pepper, bay leaf, and salt into a saucepan and bring to a boil.
3. Pour hot brine over sliced radishes. Seal the jar with a lid and store it in the refrigerator.

50. Pickled Sweet Peppers

Preparation Time: 10 minutes
Cooking Time: 5 minutes
Servings: 4

INGREDIENTS:

- 2 cups sweet peppers, sliced
- 4 garlic cloves, minced
- 2 tbsp sugar
- ¾ cup water
- ¼ cup rice vinegar
- 2 tsp salt

DIRECTION:

1. Place sliced sweet peppers into a clean jar.
2. Add vinegar, water, sugar, garlic, and salt into a small saucepan and cook until the sugar is dissolved.
3. Pour hot brine over sliced sweet peppers.
4. Seal the jar with a lid and store it in the refrigerator.

51. Pickled Asparagus

Preparation Time: 10 minutes
Cooking Time: 10 minutes
Servings: 4

INGREDIENTS:

- 1 lb fresh asparagus spears, trim ends
- ½ tsp black peppercorns
- 1 ½ tsp sugar
- 1 cup water
- 1 ½ cups vinegar
- 2 tbsp salt

DIRECTION:

1. Pack asparagus spears into jars.
2. Add water, sugar, vinegar, and salt into a saucepan and bring to a boil over medium heat.
3. Stir until sugar is dissolved.
4. Pour the hot water mixture over the asparagus. Leave ½-inch headspace.
5. Seal jar with lids.
6. Let it cool completely, then store it in the refrigerator.

Fruits

52. Yummy Blueberry Pickle

Preparation Time: 12 hours 30 minutes
Cooking Time: 15 minutes
Servings: 3 jars

INGREDIENTS:

- 3 long cinnamon sticks
- 6 cups fresh blueberries
- 1 cup brown sugar
- 1 cup white sugar
- 1 ½ cups red wine vinegar
- 1 tsp whole allspice berries
- 1 tsp whole cloves

DIRECTION:

1. Place spices – all spices, cloves, and cinnamon sticks at the center of the cheesecloth and tie it tightly. Pour vinegar into a large pan and place tied cheesecloth in the pan as well. Bring a boil and let simmer for 5 minutes for flavors of spices to infuse.
2. Stir in blueberries and cook for 5 minutes without stirring to ensure they remain intact. Remove from heat, then let stand for 12 hours.
3. Drain berries over a bowl and transfer vinegar liquid into a saucepan without cheesecloth. Stir in two cups of sugar until dissolved and simmer until it thickens into a syrup, for about 5 minutes.
4. Pack berries into prepared jars and top with sugar-vinegar syrup. Cover and process for canning.

Notes:

53. Watermelon Pickles

Preparation Time: 30 minutes
Cooking Time: 10 minutes
Servings: 4 pints

INGREDIENTS:

- 2 lb watermelon rind
- 4 cups sugar
- 2 cups white vinegar
- 2 cups water
- 1 sliced lemon
- 1 cinnamon stick
- 1 tbsp whole cloves

DIRECTION:

1. Trim dark green and pink flesh from the rind; cut into 1-inch cubes.
2. Combine ¼ pickling salt and 1 quart of water.
3. Heat and stir until the salt is dissolved.
4. Pour saltwater over the rind cubes. Leave overnight.
5. Drain and rinse cubes.
6. Place in a heavy pot or kettle.
7. Cover with cold water and cook until tender; drain.
8. In a heavy pot, combine sugar, vinegar, water, and lemon slices.
9. Put cinnamon and cloves in a cheesecloth bag and put the bag in the vinegar mixture.
10. Simmer the mixture for 10 minutes and remove the spice bag.
11. Add rind cubes to the vinegar mixture and continue cooking until the cubes are translucent.
12. Pour into hot, sterile, pint jars, dividing syrup evenly and leaving ½-inch headspace.
13. Can jars in a boiling water bath for 15 minutes.

54. Spicy Avocado Dill Pickle

Preparation Time: 15 minutes
Cooking Time: 10 minutes
Servings: 2 jars

INGREDIENTS:

- 3 avocados (not very ripe), peeled and cut into eights, lengthwise
- 2 habanero peppers
- ½ tsp habanero pepper flakes
- 2 cloves garlic, squashed and cut into two
- ½ tsp black peppercorns
- 1 tsp mustard seeds
- 2 tsp fresh dill, chopped
- ¾ cup sugar
- 2 tsp rock salt
- 1 ½ cups water
- 1 ½ cups white wine vinegar
- 1 ¼ cup distilled white vinegar

DIRECTION:

1. Add water and vinegar to a medium-sized saucepan over medium to high heat. Stir in pepper flakes, mustard seeds, black peppercorns, dill, salt, and sugar, and bring to a gentle boil. Once salt and sugar have dissolved completely, turn off the heat and let cool.
2. Meanwhile, divide avocado, garlic, and habanero peppers between two jars and pour in the cooled vinegar mixture, leaving ¼ inch of head space.
3. Tightly seal jars and refrigerate.

55. Apricot Pickle

Preparation Time: 25 minutes
Cooking Time: 5 minutes

INGREDIENTS:

- ¾ cups white wine vinegar
- ¾ cups water
- 3 tbsp turbinado sugar
- 1 tsp yellow mustard seeds
- 2 cups dried apricots
- ¼ cup dark raisins
- 1 bay leaf

DIRECTION:

1. In a small-sized non-reactive saucepan, add vinegar, water, sugar, and mustard seeds and bring to a boil, stirring occasionally.
2. Meanwhile, in the bottom of 3 (½-pint) hot sterilized jars, place apricots, raisins, and bay leaves.
3. Pour hot vinegar mixture over pear pieces, leaving about ¼-½-inch space from the top.
4. Slide a small knife around the insides of each jar to remove air bubbles.
5. Wipe any trace of food off the rims of jars with a clean, moist kitchen towel.
6. Close each jar with a lid and screw on the ring.
7. Arrange jars in a boiling water canner and process for about 10 minutes.
8. Remove jars from the water canner and place them onto a wood surface several inches apart to cool completely.
9. After cooling with your finger, press the top of each jar's lid to ensure that seal is tight.
10. Place jars of pickles in the refrigerator for up to 1 month.

56. Tart Cherry Pickle

Preparation Time: 2 hours 10 minutes
Cooking Time: 0 minutes

INGREDIENTS:

- 2 cups sour cherries with seeds
- 2 cups white wine vinegar
- 1 tsp kosher salt

DIRECTION:

1. Thoroughly wash cherries and drain them completely. Spread them on a baking tray or other wide tray and let dry in the sun for about 2 hours.
2. Pack cherries in a storage jar, sprinkle with salt and cover with vinegar. Tightly seal the jar and set it in a cool and dry jar.

Notes:

57. Grapes Pickle

Preparation Time: 25 minutes
Cooking Time: 5 minutes

INGREDIENTS:

- 1 cup white sugar
- 1 cup apple cider vinegar
- ¼ cup water
- 1 cinnamon stick
- ½ vanilla bean
- ¼ tsp cloves
- ¼ tsp black peppercorns
- 1/8 tsp yellow mustard seeds
- 1 lb red grapes, trimmed

DIRECTION:

1. In a small-sized non-reactive saucepan, add sugar, vinegar, and water over high heat and bring to a boil, stirring occasionally.
2. Meanwhile, place spices and top with grapes in the bottom of 2 (1-pint) hot sterilized jars.
3. Place vinegar mixture over green beans, leaving about ¼ to ½-inch space from the top.
4. Slide a small knife around the insides of each jar to remove air bubbles.
5. Wipe any trace of food off the rims of jars with a clean, moist kitchen towel.
6. Close each jar with a lid and screw on the ring.
7. Arrange jars in a boiling water canner and process for about 10 minutes.
8. Remove jars from the water canner and place them onto a wood surface several inches apart to cool completely.
9. After cooling with your finger, press the top of each jar's lid to ensure that seal is tight.
10. Place jars of pickles in the refrigerator for up to 1 month.

58. Currant Pickle

Preparation Time: 20 minutes
Cooking Time: 35 minutes

INGREDIENTS:

- 2 cups dried currants
- 1 cup sherry vinegar
- 2 tsp mustard seeds
- 1 tbsp fresh thyme
- ¼ cup granulated white sugar
- ¼ cup brown sugar

DIRECTION:

1. In a large-sized non-reactive saucepan, combine all ingredients over heat and bring to a boil.
2. Then adjust the heat to low and simmer for about 30 minutes, stirring occasionally.
3. Remove the saucepan of currant mixture from the heat and transfer into 1 (1-pint) hot sterilized jar.
4. Slide a small knife around the insides of each jar to remove air bubbles.
5. Wipe any trace of food off the rims of the jar with a clean, moist kitchen towel.
6. Close the jar with a lid, then screw the ring.
7. Arrange the jar in a boiling water canner and process for about 10 minutes.
8. Remove the jar from the water canner and place it onto a wooden surface several inches apart to cool completely.
9. After cooling with your finger, press the top of the jar's lid to ensure that seal is tight.
10. Place the jar of pickles in the refrigerator for up to 1 month.

59. Mustardy Garlic and Dill Pickles

Preparation Time: 20 minutes
Cooking Time: 25 minutes

INGREDIENTS:

- 1 lb fiddlehead ferns (much will be discarded after trimming)
- 4 cloves garlic, sliced
- 2 tsp dill seeds
- 2 tsp yellow mustard seed

Brine:

- 4 cups (5 percent acidity) distilled white vinegar
- 4 cups water
- ½ cup pickling salt

DIRECTION:

1. It's crucial to thoroughly clean fiddlehead ferns and gets rid of any associated brown, dry regions. Any ferns that don't appear to be green and fresh should be cut off and placed aside; you may boil those less-than-perfect ferns later for a snack.
2. After cleaning, place fiddleheads in a basin or pot with ice and water, and let them soak for an hour. Rinse with cold water after straining.
3. Fiddlehead ferns should be boiled when boiling water is added to a medium-sized pot. Set the timer for 2 minutes after the water has started to boil. Fiddleheads should be drained and placed in an ice bath to chill.
4. Bring brine ingredients to a boil in a nonstick pan for five minutes, then turn down the heat to a low simmer.
5. Divide mustard, dill, and garlic between jars that have been prepared. Fiddleheads should be packed as tightly as you can without breaking or harming jars.
6. Be very deliberate about packing the jar as tightly as you can because fiddleheads will shrink down throughout the water bath procedure.
7. Sprinkle fiddleheads with hot brine. With a 12-inch headspace, carefully pour the brine into the jar using a funnel. Clean, lint-free paper towels or wet cloths should be used to wipe jar rims, followed by a dry towel.
8. Put the canning lid on the jar and tighten the canning ring around the jar until it fits snugly. Put the lid on the canning kettle and add jars. Set timer and process in the water bath for 10 minutes when water comes to a rolling boil.
9. Using canning tongs, carefully remove jars from the water bath and set them aside for 12 hours on a towel-lined surface. Remove jar rings after 12 hours, check that all of the lids are tightly shut, then name and date jars.
10. Even while fiddleheads will taste good right away, it's preferable to let them pickle for at least 4 weeks before eating. Once the seal has been broken, refrigerate.

Notes:

60. Garlicky Scape Pickles

Preparation Time: 20 minutes
Cooking Time: 20 minutes

INGREDIENTS:

- 3 bundles of thin scapes (thinner scapes are more tender, while thick ones tend to be chewy)
- 2 cloves garlic, sliced
- 2 tsp yellow mustard seeds

Brine:

- 2 cups (5 percent acidity) distilled white vinegar
- 2 cups water
- 1 tbsp canning salt

DIRECTION:

1. Trim rough ends and clean scapes (typically, the bottom couple of inches). Similar to asparagus, they frequently have a natural point of fracture.
2. It is entirely up to you whether to let the flower bloom or cut it off. Whether you remove the bloom or leave it on has no bearing on flavor.
3. Bring brine ingredients to a boil in a nonreactive pan while stirring to dissolve the salt, then lower the heat to a low simmer. Divide mustard seeds and garlic between jars that have been prepared.
4. You can either cut scapes into little pieces or, as in my photo, wrap them in circles to pack jars. Wrapping them within a jar gives the container a very lovely and distinctive appearance.
5. Simply wrap a few scapes around your fingers at a time and carefully drop them in the jar to accomplish this.
6. Spread scapes with hot brine. With a 12-inch headspace, carefully pour the brine into the jar using a funnel.
7. Jar rims should be cleaned twice: once with a dry towel and once with a wet, clean, lint-free cloth. Put the canning lid on and tighten the canning ring around the jar until it is just-snug.
8. Put lids on jars and place them in a water bath canner. Set timer and process in the water bath for 10 minutes when water comes to a rolling boil.
9. Using canning tongs, carefully remove jars from the water bath and set them aside for 12 hours on a towel-lined surface.
10. Remove jar rings after 12 hours, check that all of the lids are tightly shut, and then name and date jars. Before tasting, let scapes pickle for 2 weeks. Once the seal has been broken, store it in the refrigerator.

Notes:

61. Scape and Garlic Pickles

Preparation Time: 20 minutes
Cooking Time: 0 minutes

INGREDIENTS:

- 3 bundles of thin scapes (thick ones tend to be chewy)
- 1 clove garlic, crushed

Brine:

- 1 tbsp kosher salt, dissolved in 2 cups of water

DIRECTION:

1. Trim rough ends, usually the bottom several inches, off scapes after washing them. Similar to asparagus, they frequently have a natural point of fracture.
2. It is entirely up to you whether to let the flower bloom or cut it off. Whether you remove the bloom or leave it on has no bearing on flavor.
3. You can either cut scapes into little pieces or, as in my photo, wrap them in circles to pack jars. By wrapping them, the jar acquires a stunning and distinctive appearance. Simply wrap a few scapes around your fingers at a time and carefully drop them in the jar to accomplish this.
4. Leave 1 to 2 inches of headroom in the jar and chop up any surplus scapes before packing them as tightly as you can in the center.
5. Pour brine over the scapes after the jar is full. Hold scapes beneath brine with a weight.
6. Cover the jar or crock with cheesecloth or another permeable covering to prevent dirt and insects from getting into your ferment. Alternately, if fermenting in a jar, place the canning cover on top and secure the ring. If using a cover, "burp" your ferment every day to let any trapped gas that is produced during fermentation out.
7. The optimal range for storage temperature is between 60 and 75°F (15 and 23°C). Keep clear jars out of direct sunlight if you're using them.
8. This ferments for 2 weeks. Make sure brine is still covering scapes and that no mold or yeast grows by checking on ferment every day. If the brine level is low, apply pressure to bring it back up to ferment. Once fermentation is finished, keep it in an airtight glass container and chill it along with the brine.

Notes:

62. Mustard with Cucumber Pickles

Preparation Time: 20 minutes
Cooking Time: 10 minutes

INGREDIENTS:

- ¼ bushel small pickling cucumbers (ideally 3" or less in size, freshly harvested within 24–48 hours)
- 2 bulbs garlic
- 6 tsp dill seeds or 1 sprig fresh dill per jar
- 6 tsp mustard seeds

Optional:

- 1 to 2 jalapeños, quartered, or 1 halved habanero pepper for extra spice

Brine:

- 8 cups (5% acidity) distilled white vinegar
- 8 cups water
- ¾ cup canning salt

DIRECTION:

1. For this recipe, use tiny pickled cucumbers. You can fill the jar with two tiers of cucumbers if you use pickling cucumbers that are 3 inches or smaller. The canned pickle's crunchiness is also a result of its small size. Pickles should always be prepared for preservation the day after purchase. Freshness plays a big part in what makes dills crunchy.
2. A 5-gallon food-grade bucket should be set aside for making pickles. The bucket should be filled with cucumbers, and then water should be added using a garden hose.
3. Carefully swirl cucumbers in water to remove any dirt or blossom blooms. Continue doing this until the water is clear. After that, immerse cucumbers in an ice bath for an hour while adding plenty of fresh water and ice to the bucket.
4. Prepare garlic while the cucumbers are in the ice bath.
5. Each cucumber should be hand-washed after cold treatment. Clean off any dirt with a vegetable brush and toss any bruised or otherwise undesirable cucumbers. After they have all been cleaned, strain them and give them a second cold water rinse.
6. Trim pickles' ends and any damaged places once they have been thoroughly cleaned. Any mushy or broken cucumbers should not be used.
7. Bring brine ingredients to a simmer in a sizable nonreactive saucepan until the salt has dissolved, then lower heat to a low simmer. Divide mustard, dill, and garlic seeds among jars.
8. Place pickles carefully within, putting them in like a puzzle. You want cucumbers to be well-packed and completely filled in a jar.
9. If necessary, slice larger cucumbers in half; however, they might not be as crisp as those left whole. When packaging jars for spicy pickles, include jalapenos among cucumbers.
10. Pour hot brine into jars with a ladle. With a 12-inch headspace, carefully pour the brine into each jar using a funnel. To get rid of air bubbles that have become stuck inside the jar, use a stainless-steel butter knife or another nonreactive object.
11. After cleaning jar rims with a clean, moist, lint-free cloth or paper towel, dry them off. Put the canning jar lid on the container and tighten the ring until it fits snugly.
12. Make sure jars are submerged in at least an inch of water before placing them in a water bath canner. Then, cover the pot. Set timer and process in the water bath for 10 minutes when water comes to a rolling boil.
13. Using canning tongs, carefully remove jars from the water bath and set them aside for 12 hours on a towel-lined surface. Remove jar rings after 12 hours, check that all of the lids are well fastened to jars, then label and date jars.
14. To give flavors a chance to mingle, I advise waiting at least two months or longer before tasting these pickles. Once the seal has been broken, store it in the refrigerator.

63. Garlic-Infused Mustard Pickles

Preparation Time: 20 minutes
Cooking Time: 0 minutes

INGREDIENTS:

- 1 to 2 lb (4 ½–5-inch) pickling cucumbers
- 10 to 15 cloves garlic or more if desired, crushed
- 2 tbsp dill seeds or 1 to 2 sprigs of fresh dill
- 1 tbsp yellow mustard seeds
- 3 jalapeños, halved (optional, if spicy pickles are desired)
- 3 to 5 grape leaves, oak leaves, raspberry leaves, or horseradish leaves (though horseradish leaves will alter the flavor of the pickle)

Brine:

- 2 tbsp kosher salt, dissolved in 4 cups water

DIRECTION:

1. After washing the pickles, place them in ice water to cool for up to an hour. Strain. Put leaves, dill, mustard, optional jalapenos, cucumbers, garlic, and other ingredients in a clean jar, crock, or another fermentation vessel.
2. Leave ferment 1 to 2 inches of headspace to prevent fermentation bubble over. Use a weight to submerge cucumbers while you pour the brine over them.
3. Install an airlock on the fermentation vessel if you're using an airlock system. If using a crock with a water seal, fill the seal with water and tighten the lid all way.
4. If using a canning jar, seal the jar with a canning lid or cover it with cheesecloth to prevent pests and dust from getting inside.
5. You will need to "burp" ferments every day to let any trapped gasses that build during fermentation out if you are tightly screwing on a canning jar cover.
6. The optimal range for storage temperature is between 60 and 75°F (15 and 23°C). Stay out of the sun's direct rays.
7. To ensure brine covers cucumbers, check on ferment every day if it's being fermented in a canning jar with a tight-fitting lid or every few days if it's being fermented in a crock, jar with an airlock, or jar covered in cheesecloth.
8. It will ferment for 14 to 30 days. They'll finish sooner if your space is warmer.
9. The brine will get hazy, and sediment will probably start accumulating on pickles or at the bottom of the ferment.
10. To know when they have "finished" fermenting, perform a taste test. Instead of tasting like raw cucumber, they need to be pickly. Put pickles in an airtight jar with brine once the fermentation process is complete, and then store them in the fridge.

Notes:

64. Spiced Dill Pickles

Preparation Time: 20 minutes
Cooking Time: 0 minutes

INGREDIENTS:

- 5 to 6 lb small cucumbers
- 6 cloves garlic, sliced
- ⅓ bunch fresh dill
- 1 tbsp yellow mustard seeds
- 1 tsp whole allspice
- 1 tbsp fresh horseradish root, sliced
- 1 to 3 grape leaves (optional)

Brine:

- 6 tbsp kosher salt dissolved in 3 quarts water

DIRECTION:

1. After washing, make a few small holes with a knife or fork at both ends of the cucumbers. Add garlic, dill, mustard seeds, allspice, horseradish root, and optional grape leaves to crock with cucumbers.
2. Pour brine over cucumbers until it reaches weights, then use weights to keep pickles in place.
3. Move fermentation to a colder area after 3 to 4 days of room temperature fermentation.
4. Any time during the fermentation process is a good time to eat pickles. Put pickles and brine in an airtight glass jar and chill until desired sourness is achieved.

65. Vinegary Pickled Beets

Preparation Time: 20 minutes
Cooking Time: 30 minutes

INGREDIENTS:

- 8 lb freshly harvested beets, small are preferred because they are more tender

Brine:

- 4 cups (5% acidity) distilled white vinegar
- 2 cups water
- 2 tsp canning salt
- 2 cups organic or non-GMO granulated sugar
- 2 tsp ground cloves

DIRECTION:

1. Cleanse beets gently with a vegetable brush. Beets should be trimmed off their leafy ends before being boiled in water. Beets should be cooked for about 25 minutes or until they are soft and readily punctured with a fork. Turn off the heat, drain, and allow to cool.
2. Trim each beet's root end once it has cooled enough to handle, then break the skin's outer layer with your hands.
3. Rub away the skin with your thumbs. It can get nasty trying to remove the skin. It is advised to have two dishes: one for peeled beets and another for skins to be removed. Over a sizable chopping board, perform this.
4. Beets should be cut into suitable sizes. You might prefer your beets to be sliced, but I like to cut mine into chunks. Fill canning jars with beets.
5. Brine components should be heated to a boil in a sizable nonreactive saucepan before being simmered at a low temperature to dissolve the salt.
6. Over beets, pour heated brine. With a 12-inch headspace, carefully pour the brine into jars using a funnel.
7. After cleaning jar rims with a clean, moist, lint-free cloth or paper towel, dry them off.
8. Put the canning lid on the jar and tighten the canning ring around the jar until it fits snugly. Cover saucepan after lowering jars into water bath canner. Set timer and process in water bath canner for 30 minutes once water bath reaches a rolling boil.
9. With the aid of canning tongs, carefully remove jars from the water bath. Lay jars flat for 12 to 24 hours without touching them.
10. Remove rings from jars after 12 to 24 hours, when they have completely cooled, and check to see whether all lids are tightly fastened to jars. Then, label and date jars. Once the seal has been broken, store it in the refrigerator.

66. Pickled Watermelon Rinds

Preparation Time: 20 minutes
Cooking Time: 20 minutes

INGREDIENTS:

- Watermelon rind, peeled
- 1 cinnamon stick

Overnight soak:

- ¼ cup pickling salt
- 3 cups water

Brine:

- 1 cup (5% acidity) distilled white vinegar
- 1 cup water
- 1 cup organic or non-GMO granulated sugar
- 1 tsp ground clove

DIRECTION:

1. Watermelon should be cleaned, dried, and sliced into quarters. Remove juicy pink fruit with a spoon, doing your best to separate the pink flesh from the peel. A spoon works well for scraping.
2. Peel the watermelon's rough green outer covering with a potato peeler. Cut the watermelon rind into 1-inch strips and then again into 1-inch squares once you have a prepared, light-colored rind. Spend the night in a saltwater bath.
3. Rinse the rind many times in cold water the following day to get rid of salt water. Bring vinegar, water, sugar, and clove to a boil in a medium pot with a heavy bottom.
4. Stirring constantly, boil for 5 minutes. Fill a quart jar with rinsed watermelon rind until it is 1 inch below the jar's top. Along with the watermelon rind, insert the cinnamon stick.
5. Over rind, ladle heated brine. To carefully transfer brine to the jar, use a funnel. Leave a headspace of 14 inches. Clean the jar's rim by wiping it with a damp paper towel or lint-free towel, followed by a dry towel. The canning lid should now be on the jar, and the canning ring should be snugly fastened.
6. When the water bath reaches a rolling boil, carefully lower jars into it, cover with lid, and process in the water bath for 10 minutes.
7. Using canning tongs, carefully remove jars from the water bath and set them aside for 12 hours on a towel-lined surface. Remove jar rings after 12 hours, check that all of the lids are well fastened to jars, then label and date jars. Once the seal has been broken, refrigerate.

Notes:

67. Spiced Berries with Bay Pickles

Preparation Time: 20 minutes
Cooking Time: 10 minutes

INGREDIENTS:

- 10 lb cucumbers, 3 to 4 inches in length
- 2 tbsp black peppercorns
- 2 tbsp mustard seeds
- 2 tbsp coriander seeds
- 2 tbsp dill seeds
- 1 tbsp allspice berries
- 12 bay leaves, crumbled
- 4 cups white vinegar
- 4 cups water
- ½ cup canning salt
- 1 grape leaf per jar
- 2 heads of dill per jar
- 2 cloves crushed garlic per jar
- A few flakes of crushed chili peppers per jar (optional)

DIRECTION:

1. Cucumbers should be scrubbed with a vegetable brush before soaking for 2 to 6 hours in ice water.
2. Mix peppercorns, mustard, coriander, dill, allspice, and crumbled bay leaves in a small bowl. Mix well. This will be your spice blend.
3. In a stockpot, combine white vinegar, water, and canning salt. Bring to a rolling boil for 5 minutes.
4. Each jar should have a grape leaf in the bottom. Then add 6 to 8 cucumbers, a tbsp of your spice mixture, fresh dill, and garlic to each jar. Depending on your preferences, you can prepare cucumbers whole or chop them into spears.
5. Over the contents of each jar, pour hot brine.
6. Process your jars for 10 minutes in a water bath canner while accounting for altitude.
7. Remove jars from the canner for a crisper pickle as soon as possible.
8. Waiting 7 to 10 days before opening a jar for optimum results is the difficult part.

68. Mustardy Turmeric Pickles

Preparation Time: 20 minutes
Cooking Time: 10 minutes

INGREDIENTS:

- 5 to 7 lb (4- to 6-inch) cucumbers, cut into ¼-inch slices
- 2 lb white onion, thinly sliced into rings
- ½ cup canning salt
- 3 cups white vinegar
- 2 cups white sugar
- 2 tbsp mustard seeds
- 2 tsp ground turmeric
- 2 tsp celery seeds
- 1 tsp ground ginger
- 1 tsp peppercorns
- 1 grape leaf per jar

DIRECTION:

1. Slices of cucumber and onion should be layered in a big glass dish with canning salt.
2. Salted vegetables should be covered with ice cubes and left in the refrigerator for 2 hours.
3. In a colander, drain vegetables, then rinse and repeat.
4. In a sizable saucepot, combine all ingredients, excluding grape leaves, and bring to a boil.
5. If used, place one grape leaf in the bottom of each of your sanitized jars. Add cucumbers and onions on top.
6. Leaving a headspace of 12 inches, pour hot brine over the contents of jars.
7. In a water bath canner, process jars for 10 minutes while accounting for altitude.
8. Like other pickles, these also get better with age. Do not open them for at least a week.

69. Vinegary Carrot with Dill Pickles

Preparation Time: 20 minutes
Cooking Time: 10 minutes

INGREDIENTS:

- 6 lb carrots, peeled and trimmed to fit your jars
- 4 cups water
- 4 cups apple cider vinegar
- ½ cup brown sugar
- 4 tbsp canning salt
- 1 tbsp dill seeds
- ½ tbsp black peppercorns
- 6 cloves garlic, crushed

DIRECTION:

1. Your carrots should be speared. Your carrot chunks' sizes will depend on the size of your jars.
2. Bring water, vinegar, sugar, and salt to a boil in a saucepan.
3. Following the addition of additional spices evenly throughout sanitized jars, tightly pack carrots into each jar.
4. With a 12-inch headspace, pour the brine over the contents of the jars.
5. Clean the jar's lip, secure the top, and boil carrot pickles for 10 minutes while accounting for altitude.

70. Garlicky Cucumber with Bay Pickles

Preparation Time: 20 minutes
Cooking Time: 30 minutes

INGREDIENTS:

- 7 lb small pickling (Kirby) cucumbers
- 3 tbsp pickling spice
- 8 cups distilled white vinegar
- 8 cups water
- 1 cup sugar
- 1 cup pickling and canning salt
- 8 fresh grape or maple leaves
- 8 bay leaves
- 8 garlic cloves, peeled but whole
- 8 dill flower heads or 7 tsp dill seeds
- 4 tbsp mustard seeds

DIRECTION:

1. Clean jars should be lying in hot water because this recipe must be hot-packed. Put lids, rings, 1 tbsp distilled white vinegar, and enough water to cover them in a smaller pot. After 5 minutes of boiling, turn off the heat and set the pot aside.
2. Simply cut off $1/16$ an inch of each cucumber's blossom ends if keeping them whole (blossoms contain an enzyme that causes excessive softening of pickles). Cut them into circles that are 14 inches thick if slicing.
3. Place pickling spice in the center of a cheesecloth square of 5 inches. To create a bag, gather the cloth's corners. Use butcher's thread to tie the spice bag's top shut.
4. In a large stockpot, combine vinegar, water, sugar, pickling salt, and a spice bag. Over medium-high heat, bring to a boil while frequently swirling to help sugar and salt dissolve. To incorporate spices into the brine, lower the heat to a simmer and let it go for 15 minutes. Take out and throw away the spice bag.
5. On a chopping board, place hot jars. For pints, fill each jar with one grape leaf, one bay leaf, one garlic clove, one dill flower head (or 1 tsp dill seeds), and one and ½ tbsp mustard seeds. 2 grape leaves, 2 bay leaves, 2 garlic cloves, two dill flower heads (or 2 tsp dill seeds), and 1 tbsp mustard seeds should be added to each quart-sized jar. Cucumbers should be tightly packed into jars, leaving 1-inch headspace.
6. Maintaining 1-inch headspace, pour boiling brine over cucumbers using a funnel. Eliminate any air bubbles and, if necessary, add more brine to maintain 1-inch headspace.
7. Use a warm towel dipped in distilled white vinegar to wipe the rim of each jar. Each jar should have a lid and ring attached. Hand-tighten.
8. Place jars in water bather, ensuring that there is at least 1 inch of water covering each jar.
9. Turn the heat to high and add 2 tsp distilled white vinegar to the water. Process quarts for 20 minutes and pints for 15 minutes after bringing the canner to a boil.
10. Before setting your timer, make sure to wait until the water is fully rolling to boil. Before removing jars from the canner after processing, give them 5 minutes.

71. Gingered Turmeric Pickles

Preparation Time: 20 minutes
Cooking Time: 10 minutes

INGREDIENTS:

- 4 lb pickling (Kirby) cucumbers, cut into ¼-inch-thick rounds (12 cups)
- 6 to 8 small sweet onions, thinly sliced (6 cups)
- ⅔ cup pickling and canning salt
- 4 cups apple cider vinegar
- 2 ½ cups packed light or dark brown sugar
- 3 tbsp mustard seeds
- 1 tbsp ground ginger
- 2 tsp ground turmeric
- 1 tsp celery seeds

DIRECTION:

1. Clean jars should be lying in hot water because this recipe must be hot-packed. Put lids, rings, 1 tablespoon of distilled white vinegar, and enough water to cover them in a smaller pot. After 5 minutes of boiling, turn off the heat and set the pot aside.
2. Combine cucumbers, onions, and pickling salt in a big basin. Mix well. For 2 hours, at room temperature, cover with cold water.
3. Combine celery seeds, mustard seeds, ginger, turmeric, and vinegar in a sizable stockpot. Stirring to help the sugar dissolve, bring to a boil over medium-high heat.
4. Drain cucumbers and onions in a big colander in the sink, then rinse them for about 5 minutes under cool running water. Shake cucumbers and onions well to remove any extra water. To brine in the stockpot, add rinsed and drained cucumbers and onions. Regain a boil after thoroughly blending for one minute, boil.
5. On a chopping board, place hot jars. Fill each jar with cucumber and onion mixture, allowing a 1-inch headspace, using a funnel and a slotted spoon. Sprinkle vegetables with hot pickling brine, leaving 1-inch headspace. To keep 12-inch headspace, remove air bubbles and, if necessary, add more brine.
6. Use a warm towel dipped in distilled white vinegar to wipe the rim of each jar. Each jar should have a lid and ring attached. Hand-tighten.
7. Place jars in a water bather, making sure that there is at least 1 inch of water in the bottom of each jar. Turn the heat to high and add 2 tsp distilled white vinegar to the water. Pints are processed for 10 minutes after coming to a boil. Make sure to wait until the water is fully rolling to boil before setting your timer. Before removing jars from the canner after processing, give them 5 minutes.

Notes:

72. Pickled Red Cabbage

Preparation Time: 20 minutes
Cooking Time: 15 minutes

INGREDIENTS:

- 7 ½ lb red cabbages (3 medium heads), quartered, cored, and finely shredded (12 cups)
- ½ cup pickling and canning salt
- 2 tbsp pickling spice
- 4 cinnamon sticks, broken
- 4 cups apple cider vinegar
- 1 ½ cups sugar

DIRECTION:

1. Layer pickling salt with cabbage in a big bowl until it is completely covered. Mix thoroughly and cover. Place the mixture in the refrigerator for up to 12 hours.
2. Clean jars should be lying in hot water because this recipe must be hot-packed. Put lids, rings, 1 tbsp distilled white vinegar, and enough water to cover them in a smaller pot. After 5 minutes of boiling, turn off the heat and set the pot aside.
3. To get rid of as much salt as possible, rinse and drain cabbage thoroughly in a colander in the sink. Shake off the cabbage's extra water firmly. In quarts, lightly pack cabbage, leaving 1-inch headspace.
4. A 5-inch square of cheesecloth should have pickling spice and broken cinnamon sticks in the center. To create a bag, gather the cloth's corners. Use butcher's thread to tie the spice bag's top shut.
5. Combine vinegar, sugar, and spice bag in a large stockpot. Over medium-high heat, bring to a boil while frequently stirring to dissolve sugar. To incorporate spices into the brine, lower the heat and simmer on low for 15 minutes. Get rid of heat. Take out and throw away the spice bag.
6. On a chopping board, place hot jars. Pour heated brine over cabbage using a funnel. Use an air bubble removal tool to press down on the cabbage to release any trapped air and maintain 1-inch headspace.
7. Place jars in a water bather, making sure that there is at least 1 inch of water in the bottom of each jar. Turn the heat to high and add 2 tsp distilled white vinegar to the water. For 20 minutes, process pints after bringing them to a boil. Make sure to wait until the water is fully rolling to boil before setting your timer. Before removing jars from the canner after processing, give them 5 minutes.

Notes:

73. Onion with Pickled Beets

Preparation Time: 20 minutes
Cooking Time: 15 minutes

INGREDIENTS:

- 3 tbsp pickling spice
- 4 ½ lb beets (12 to 14 medium)
- 2 large Vidalia onions, sliced
- 2 ½ cups distilled white vinegar
- 1 cup water
- 1 cup sugar

DIRECTION:

1. Clean jars should be lying in hot water because this recipe must be hot-packed. Put lids, rings, 1 tbsp distilled white vinegar, and enough water to cover them in a smaller pot. After 5 minutes of boiling, turn off the heat and set the pot aside.
2. In the center of a cheesecloth square of 5 inches, place pickling spice. To create a bag, gather the cloth's corners. Use butcher's thread to tie the spice bag's top shut.
3. Each beet should retain its 2-inch stem and root after being thoroughly washed. In a sizable stockpot, add beets and cover with water. Beets should be cooked for 30 minutes, or until they begin to soften.
4. Hot beets should be put in a bowl of cold water in the sink using a slotted spoon. Simply rub beet with your thumbs in the palm of your palms as it cools to remove the skin.
5. Quarter beets after removing all of the roots and stems. About ten cups of quartered beets will be available. Place aside.
6. Combine onions, vinegar, water, sugar, and a spice bag in a big stockpot. Over medium-high heat, bring to a boil while stirring until sugar dissolves. For 15 minutes, simmer on a lower heat.
7. Take out and throw away the spice bag. Bring brine back to a boil over heat after adding prepared beets. When it boils, turn off the heat and start filling jars.
8. On a chopping board, place hot jars. Beets should be added to each jar with a generous 12-inch headspace using a funnel and a slotted spoon.
9. Make sure to leave a 1-inch headspace as you pour boiling brine over the beets. If there are any air bubbles, remove them and, if necessary, add more brine to maintain a 1-inch headspace.
10. Use a warm towel dipped in distilled white vinegar to wipe the rim of each jar. Each jar should have a lid and ring attached. Hand-tighten.
11. Place the jars in the water bather, making sure that there are 2 inches of water in the bottom of each one. Turn the heat to high and add 2 tsp distilled white vinegar to the water.
12. Process quarts for 40 minutes and pints for 30 minutes after bringing them to a boil. Make sure to wait until the water is fully rolling to boil before setting your timer. Before removing jars from the canner after processing, give them 5 minutes.

Notes:

74. Asparagus with Pickled Mustard

Preparation Time: 20 minutes
Cooking Time: 5 minutes

INGREDIENTS:

- 5 cups distilled white vinegar
- 5 cups water
- ½ cup pickling and canning salt
- 6 fresh grape or maple leaves
- 6 garlic cloves, peeled but whole
- 3 tsp dill seeds or 6 dill flower heads
- 3 tsp mustard seeds
- 3 tsp red pepper flakes (optional)
- 7 lb asparagus, stem ends trimmed to fit the jar

DIRECTION:

1. Clean jars should be lying in hot water because this recipe must be hot-packed. Put lids and rings, 1 tbsp distilled white vinegar, and enough water to cover them in a smaller pot. After 5 minutes of boiling, turn off the heat and set the pot aside.
2. Combine vinegar, water, and pickling salt in a sizable stockpot. Stirring continuously until salt dissolves, bring to a boil over medium-high heat. 5 minutes of boiling. Heat has been removed; set aside.
3. On a chopping board, place hot jars. For pints, fill each jar with 1 grape leaf, 1 garlic clove, 1 dill seed or dill flower, 1 tsp mustard seeds, and 1 tsp pepper flakes (if used). Double all amounts for quarts.
4. Leaving a 1-inch headspace, raw pack asparagus spears into jars with tips facing down. If the stem ends encroach on headspace, cut them off.
5. After packing, place the jars back on the cutting board. To eliminate any air bubbles, gently tap the bottom of each jar on the cutting board. If additional brine is required to maintain 12-inch headspace, do so.
6. Use a warm towel dipped in distilled white vinegar to wipe the rim of each jar. Each jar should have a lid and ring attached. Hand-tighten.
7. Place jars in a water bather, ensuring that there is at least 1 inch of water in the bottom of each jar. Turn the heat to high and add 2 tsp distilled white vinegar to the water. Process quarts for 15 minutes and pints for 10 minutes after bringing them to a boil. Make sure to wait until the water is fully rolling to boil before setting your timer. Before removing jars from the canner after processing, give them 5 minutes.

Notes:

75. Pickled Brussels Sprouts with Vinegar

Preparation Time: 20 minutes
Cooking Time: 5 minutes

INGREDIENTS:

- 6 cups distilled white vinegar
- 2 cups water
- ½ cup pickling and canning salt
- 15 to 20 garlic cloves, peeled and crushed
- 2 ½ tsp red pepper flakes
- 3 lb Brussels sprouts

DIRECTION:

1. Clean jars should be lying in hot water because this recipe must be hot-packed. Put lids, rings, 1 tbsp distilled white vinegar, and enough water to cover them in a smaller pot. After 5 minutes of boiling, turn off the heat and set the pot aside.
2. In a large pot, combine vinegar, water, and pickling salt. Stirring continuously until salt dissolves, bring to a boil over medium-high heat. 5 minutes of boiling. Heat has been removed; set aside.
3. On a chopping board, place hot jars. Add 3 garlic cloves and ½ tsp red pepper flakes to each pint-sized jar. Add 2 garlic cloves and ¼ tsp pepper flakes to each half-pint jar.
4. Whole Brussels sprouts should be packed into jars, with larger sprouts being chopped in half and a wide 12-inch headspace.
5. After packing, place the jars back on the cutting board. Pour heated brine over Brussels sprouts using a funnel, allowing a 1-inch headspace. If required, add more brine and gently tap the jar bottom on the cutting board to remove any air bubbles, making sure to keep 12-inch headspace.
6. Use a warm towel dipped in distilled white vinegar to wipe the rim of each jar. Each jar should have a lid and ring attached. Hand-tighten.
7. Place jars in water bather, making sure that there is at least 1 inch of water covering each jar. Turn the heat to high and add 2 tsp distilled white vinegar to the water. Both pints and half-pints should be processed for 10 minutes after bringing them to a boil. Make sure to wait until the water is fully rolling to boil before setting your timer. Before removing jars from the canner after processing, give them 5 minutes.

Notes:

76. Lemony Pickled Peaches

Preparation Time: 20 minutes
Cooking Time: 5 minutes

INGREDIENTS:

- 4 cups sugar
- 1 ½ cups apple cider vinegar
- 1 ½ cups water
- ¼ tsp pickling and canning salt
- Zest of 1 lemon
- 2 ½ tbsp whole cloves
- 7 lb peaches (25 medium), peeled, halved, and pitted
- 7 cinnamon sticks

DIRECTION:

1. Clean jars should be lying in hot water because this recipe must be hot-packed. Put lids, rings, 1 tbsp distilled white vinegar, and enough water to cover them in a smaller pot. After 5 minutes of boiling, turn off the heat and set the pot aside.
2. Combine sugar, vinegar, water, pickling salt, and lemon zest in a big stockpot. Over medium-high heat, bring to a boil while frequently swirling to help sugar and salt dissolve. After 5 minutes of simmering on low heat, turn off the heat.
3. On a chopping board, place hot jars. For each quart and a pint of liquid, add 1 tsp of cloves. Cut-side down, place peaches in jars, leaving 1-inch headspace. Make sure cinnamon sticks are visible through the jar's side when you insert one stick into each quart and a half stick into each pint.
4. Fill peaches with hot brine, leaving 1-inch headspace, using a funnel. Eliminate any air bubbles and, if necessary, add more brine to maintain 1-inch headspace.
5. Use a warm towel dipped in distilled white vinegar to wipe the rim of each jar. Each jar should have a lid and ring attached. Hand-tighten.
6. Place jars in a water bather, making sure that there is at least 1 inch of water in the bottom of each jar. Turn the heat to high and add 2 teaspoons of distilled white vinegar to the water. Quarts should be processed for 20 minutes and pints for 15 minutes after bringing them to a boil. Make sure to wait until the water is fully rolling to boil before setting your timer. Before removing jars from the canner after processing, give them 5 minutes.

Notes:

77. Celery with Cauliflower Pickles

Preparation Time: 20 minutes
Cooking Time: 20 minutes

INGREDIENTS:

- 1 cup pickling and canning salt
- 4 quarts water (16 cups)
- 3 cucumbers, cut into 1-inch chunks (2 cups)
- 2 bell peppers, coarsely chopped (2 cups)
- 1 head cauliflower, cut into florets (3 cups)
- 6 green tomatoes, chopped (3 cups)
- 6 carrots, peeled, halved, and cut into 1-inch chunks (3 cups)
- 2 celery stalks, cut into 1-inch chunks (1 cup)
- 1 onion, sliced (1 cup)
- 6 cups apple cider vinegar
- 2 cups packed light brown sugar
- 2 tbsp ground turmeric
- 2 tbsp celery seeds
- 2 tbsp mustard seeds

DIRECTION:

1. In a large bowl, mix pickling salt and water, stirring until the salt is dissolved. Add cucumbers, bell peppers, cauliflower, tomatoes, carrots, celery, and onion, and refrigerate for 8 hours or overnight.
2. Clean jars should be lying in hot water because this recipe must be hot-packed. Put lids and rings, 1 tbsp distilled white vinegar, and enough water to cover them in a smaller pot. After 5 minutes of boiling, turn off the heat and set the pot aside.
3. In a large pot, combine vinegar, brown sugar, turmeric, celery seeds, and mustard seeds. Bring to a boil over medium-high heat, stirring until sugar is dissolved. Reduce heat to medium and boil gently for 5 minutes.
4. Empty a bowl of refrigerated vegetables into a colander in the sink and drain well. Transfer vegetables to stockpot of hot brine and heat over heat for 15 minutes to heat through, stirring often.
5. On a chopping board, place hot jars. Using a funnel and a slotted spoon, fill each jar with vegetables, leaving a ½-inch headspace. Ladle hot brine over vegetables, maintaining ½-inch headspace. If required, add more brine and gently tap the jar bottom on the cutting board to remove any air bubbles, making sure to keep 12-inch headspace.
6. Use a warm towel dipped in distilled white vinegar to wipe the rim of each jar. Each jar should have a lid and ring attached. Hand-tighten.
7. Place jars in a water bather, ensuring that there is at least 1 inch of water in the bottom of each jar. Turn the heat to high and add 2 tsp distilled white vinegar to the water. Quarts should be processed for 20 minutes and pints for 15 minutes after bringing them to a boil.
8. Before setting your timer, make sure to wait until the water is fully rolling to boil. Before removing jars from the canner after processing, give them 5 minutes.

Notes:

78. Pickled Apples

Preparation Time: 10 minutes
Cooking Time: 7 minutes

INGREDIENTS:

- ¾ lb apples
- 1 cup apple cider vinegar
- ½ cup water
- ¾ cup sugar
- 1 (4-inch) cinnamon stick, broken
- 1 tsp allspice berries
- ½ tsp black peppercorns
- 3 whole cloves

DIRECTION:

1. Halve and core apples, and then thinly slice them.
2. In a nonreactive pot, combine the remaining ingredients and bring them to a boil. Reduce heat, stirring until sugar dissolves.
3. Add apples and return the brine to a boil. Reduce heat, cover, and simmer apples for 3 minutes.
4. Transfer apples to a jar or bowl and set them on the counter until they come to room temperature. Cover apples with a nonreactive lid and store them refrigerated for at least 8 hours. Store them for up to 1 month.

A CLOSER LOOK: There is often an abundance of apples available in the fall, but not all apples are created equally, especially when it comes to cooking. Look for Gala, Granny Smith, Pink Lady, Braeburn, or Fuji apples. All are good choices that hold up well to heat processing.

79. Pickled Pears

Preparation Time: 10 minutes
Cooking Time: 30 minutes

INGREDIENTS:

- 2 lb pears
- 1 ½ cups sugar
- 1 ½ cups water
- 1 ½ cups white vinegar
- 1 tsp cloves
- 3 cinnamon sticks
- 1 (1-inch) piece ginger, peeled and thinly sliced

DIRECTION:

1. Halve and core pears or, if desired, leave them whole. Treat for browning (see here), and pack into jars.
2. In a nonreactive pot, combine sugar, water, and vinegar. Bring to a boil.
3. Divide cloves, cinnamon sticks, and ginger evenly between jars. Pour hot brine over pears, use a nonreactive utensil to remove air bubbles, and leave ½ inch of headspace. Wipe rims and cap jars using two-piece canning lids.
4. Process in a boiling-water bath for 10 minutes. Keep jars in a cool, dark, and dry location for at least 1 week before eating.

Notes:

80. Pickled Peaches

Preparation Time: 10 minutes
Cooking Time: 30 minutes

INGREDIENTS:

- 2 tsp mixed pickling spice
- ¼ tsp red chili pepper flakes
- 1 cinnamon stick
- 4 cups water
- 2 cups white vinegar
- 1 ½ cups sugar
- 1 ½ tsp pickling salt
- 2 lb peaches, peeled, quartered, and pitted

DIRECTION:

1. In a nonreactive pot, combine mixed pickling spice, red chili pepper flakes, cinnamon sticks, water, vinegar, sugar, and salt. Bring to a boil, stirring to dissolve sugar and salt. Lower heat to a simmer.
2. Add peaches and continue to simmer until peaches are just tender for about 20 minutes.
3. Transfer peaches to a jar, covering with pickling liquid. Cool to room temperature and then refrigerate for 1 day before eating.

A CLOSER LOOK: To remove peach skin and skins of other thick-skinned fruits, cut an "X" in the skin with a paring knife. Blanch peaches in boiling water briefly, about 30 seconds, and immediately transfer them to an ice-cold bath. Skins should slip off easily after this. If they don't, blanch them a little longer and try again.

81. Pickled Blueberries

Preparation Time: 10 minutes
Cooking Time: 12 minutes

INGREDIENTS:

- 1 cup red wine vinegar
- 1 cinnamon stick, broken
- 3 whole cloves
- 2 whole star anise
- 2 whole cardamom pods
- 1 (1-inch) piece ginger, peeled and thinly sliced
- ½ cup sugar

DIRECTION:

1. Wash and pick through blueberries, removing any that are mushy or bruised.
2. Pour vinegar into a nonreactive pot. Create a spice bag using a cheesecloth piece, and add a cinnamon stick, cloves, star anise, cardamom, and ginger. Simmer over low heat, covered, for 5 minutes.
3. Gently add blueberries to the pot and cook until just heated through. Shake the pot to mix berries instead of stirring to keep the berries whole.
4. Remove the pot from heat, cover it, and let it sit for 12 hours at room temperature.
5. The following day, using a slotted spoon, remove berries from the liquid and transfer them to a sterile pint jar.
6. Add sugar to spiced vinegar. Bring liquid to a boil, stirring to dissolve sugar. Boil syrup until it just begins to thicken, about 3 to 4 minutes. Pour hot liquid over the berries and seal the jar using a two-piece lid.
7. Refrigerate berries for at least 2 days before eating.

82. Minty Pickled Strawberries

Preparation Time: 10 minutes
Cooking Time: 10 minutes

INGREDIENTS:

- 2 pints strawberries
- 10 to 12 fresh mint leaves
- ¾ cup balsamic vinegar
- ¼ cup rice vinegar
- ½ cup water
- ½ cup sugar
- 2 whole star anise
- 2 whole cloves
- 1 cinnamon stick, broken
- 1 (1-inch) piece of ginger, peeled and sliced

DIRECTION:

1. Wash and hull strawberries. Halve them if desired. Pack strawberries and mint leaves into a sterile pint jar.
2. In a nonreactive pot, combine kinds of vinegar, water, sugar, star anise, cloves, cinnamon stick, and ginger. Bring to a boil, then turn off the heat. Remove star anise from spiced vinegar and pour the liquid over the strawberries. Cap jar with a nonreactive lid.
3. Refrigerate strawberries for at least 2 days before serving.

83. Sweet Pickled Cherries

Preparation Time: 10 minutes
Cooking Time: 10 minutes

INGREDIENTS:

- 1 lb sweet or sour cherries, stemmed and pitted
- 1 ½ cups white vinegar
- ¾ cup sugar
- Seeds of 1 cardamom pod
- 1 cinnamon stick

DIRECTION:

1. Place cherries in a nonreactive bowl and cover them with vinegar. Cover the bowl and let cherries stand at room temperature for 3 days.
2. Strain vinegar into a nonreactive pot. Add sugar, cardamom seeds, and a cinnamon stick. Boil liquid, then turn it down and simmer for 10 minutes.
3. Pour hot liquid over the cherries, and then use a nonreactive lid to cap the jar tightly. Keep jars in a cool, dark, and dry location for at least 1 month before eating.

84. Brined Cherries

Preparation Time: 10 minutes
Cooking Time: 10 minutes

INGREDIENTS:

- ¾ lb cherries
- 2 hot chile peppers, split lengthwise
- 2 garlic cloves, crushed
- ¼ tsp black peppercorns
- 1 bay leaf
- 1 tbsp pickling salt
- 1 ½ cups water

DIRECTION:

1. Place cherries, chile peppers, garlic, peppercorns, and bay leaf in a pint jar.
2. In a bowl, dissolve salt in water and pour this brine over the cherries. Cap jar loosely with a nonreactive lid and leave at room temperature for 1 week.
3. Transfer to refrigerator, where they will keep for 1 month.

85. Pickled Plums

Preparation Time: 10 minutes
Cooking Time: 10 minutes

INGREDIENTS:

- 2 lb Italian plums
- 1 ½ cups red wine vinegar
- ½ cup sugar
- 1 cinnamon stick, broken in half
- 4 whole cloves
- 1 tsp cardamom seeds
- 1 (2-inch) piece ginger, peeled and thinly sliced

DIRECTION:

1. Use a skewer to poke each plum three times. In a nonreactive pot, combine vinegar and sugar. Bring to a boil, stirring to dissolve sugar. Add plums to the pot and lower the heat to a simmer. Continue to cook for a few minutes until the plums are heated through.
2. While plums are cooking, divide cinnamon sticks, cloves, cardamom seeds, and ginger between two sterile quart jars.
3. Transfer plums to jars and ladle in syrup to cover them. Cap jars using nonreactive lids and store plums in a cool, dark, and dry location for 1 month before opening. Once opened, refrigerate.

86. Spiced Watermelon Pickles

Preparation Time: 10 minutes
Cooking Time: 10 minutes

INGREDIENTS:

- 5 ½ cups water, divided
- ¼ cup pickling salt
- 6 cups prepared watermelon rind
- 1 ½ cups white vinegar
- 2 cups sugar
- 2 cinnamon sticks
- ½ tsp whole cloves
- ½ tsp allspice

DIRECTION:

1. In a nonreactive bowl, pour 4 cups water and salt, stirring to combine. Add watermelon rind and use a small plate to hold pieces down in brine. Leave at room temperature overnight.
2. The following day, drain the watermelon rind. Fill a bowl with water again, and drain again.
3. In a nonreactive pot, combine 1 ½ cups water and the remaining ingredients and bring them to a boil. Turn down the heat and simmer for 10 minutes. Add watermelon rind pieces and turn off the heat. Leave syrup in the pot for up to 24 hours.
4. Bring the mixture back to a boil and simmer the rinds for 5 to 10 minutes, until they become translucent. Remove pot from heat.
5. Pack watermelon rinds and syrup into three-pint jars. Cap jars using two-piece canning lids. Process in a boiling-water bath for 10 minutes. Store jars in a cool, dark, and dry location.

Notes

87. Lacto-Fermented Watermelon Pickles

Preparation Time: 10 minutes
Cooking Time: 10 minutes

INGREDIENTS:

- 4 cups prepared watermelon rind
- 1-quart water
- 2 tbsp pickling salt

DIRECTION:

1. Pack watermelon rind into a quart jar.
2. Mix water and salt in a bowl until salt is dissolved. Pour this brine over watermelon rinds. Use a nonreactive utensil to check for air bubbles and, if necessary, use a small weight to hold watermelon rinds below the surface. Loosely cap the jar using a nonreactive lid.
3. Leave the jar at room temperature for 5 to 7 days, or until an appetizing flavor and texture have been produced. Close the jar tightly and transfer it to the refrigerator.

88. Pickled Figs

Preparation Time: 10 minutes
Cooking Time: 20 minutes

INGREDIENTS:

- 2 cups sugar
- 4 cups water
- 1 cinnamon stick
- 1 tsp whole cloves
- 1 tsp whole allspice
- 2 ½ lb firm but ripe figs
- 1 ½ cups apple cider vinegar

DIRECTION:

1. In a nonreactive pot, combine sugar, water, cinnamon stick, cloves, and allspice. Bring to a boil, constantly stirring to dissolve sugar. Lower heat to a simmer and carefully add figs. Stir figs gently as they simmer for about 20 minutes until they are tender. Add vinegar and continue to cook until the liquid begins simmering again.
2. Ladle figs into four-pint jars and cover with syrup, leaving ½ inch of headspace.
3. Process in a boiling-water bath for 15 minutes. Store jars in a cool, dry, dark location.

A CLOSER LOOK: Figs are loaded with fiber and are a great addition to the diet. When looking for figs for pickling, be sure to select ones that are firm but ripe without blemishes. In most regions of the country, this is not a problem, as they are most often picked when underripe to allow for transport.

89. Pickled Lemons

Preparation Time: 10 minutes
Cooking Time: 12 minutes

INGREDIENTS:

- 2 small lemons
- 1 tsp cumin seeds
- 1 tsp black peppercorns
- 1 tbsp pickling salt
- 3 tbsp lemon juice
- 1 cup brown sugar

A CLOSER LOOK: When using whole lemons, select organic lemons, as commercial lemons are waxed, dyed, and have considerable pesticide and fungicide residues.

DIRECTION:

1. Cut lemons in half lengthwise and then thinly slice them. Grind cumin and peppercorns in a spice grinder or with a mortar and pestle. Mix spices together with salt. In a half-pint jar, layer lemon slices with a salt-spice mixture, packing them down as you go. Cover lemons with lemon juice. Put the jar in a warm location and let it sit for at least 7 days.
2. Pour juice from the jar into a nonreactive pan, pressing as you do to extract more juice from the lemons. Add brown sugar and slowly bring mixture to a simmer, stirring to dissolve sugar. Add lemons and simmer for an additional 10 minutes.
3. Pack lemons and juices back into a half-pint jar, cap the jar tightly and leave the jar at room temperature for 1 month. Transfer the jar to the refrigerator. Refrigerated it can be stored for several months.

Kimchi, Tsukemono, and Other Pickles from East Asia

90. Cabbage, Carrot, Cucumber, and Broccoli Kimchi

Preparation Time: 10 minutes
Cooking Time: 3 to 6 days

INGREDIENTS:

- 3 tbsp, plus 1 tsp pickling salt, divided
- 6 cups water
- 1 lb Chinese cabbage, cut into 1-inch squares
- 2 cucumbers, peeled and julienned
- 3 carrots, peeled and julienned
- 2 small heads of broccoli, divided into florets and stems cut into ¼-inch rounds
- 6 scallions, cut into rounds
- 1 tbsp minced ginger
- 2 tbsp Korean ground dried hot pepper
- 1 tsp sugar

DIRECTION:

1. In a nonreactive bowl, dissolve 3 tbsp salt in water. Place cabbage and cucumbers in water and weigh them down using a plate. Leave the bowl, covered with a kitchen towel, at room temperature for 12 hours.
2. Strain cabbage and cucumbers, reserving brine. Transfer the mixture to another bowl and mix it together with all remaining ingredients, including the remaining 1 tsp salt.
3. Pack vegetable mixture into a 2-quart jar. Cover vegetables with reserved brine until the cabbage is submerged. Use a small weight to hold the cabbage down, or pour the remaining brine into a food-safe zip-top bag and press this into the mouth of the jar to weigh down the cabbage.
4. Put the jar in a location that stays around 68°F, and leave it to ferment for 3 to 6 days, or until soured to your liking.
5. Remove the weight and close the jar tightly with a nonreactive lid. Keep it in the refrigerator. Transfer the jar to the refrigerator. Refrigerated it can be stored for several months.

Notes

91. Kale and Carrot Kimchi

Preparation Time: 10 minutes
Cooking Time: 4 hours

INGREDIENTS:

- 4 lb kale, cleaned, stalks removed, and cut into 2-inch squares
- 1 tbsp kosher salt
- ¾ cup water
- ¼ cup sugar
- 2 tbsp minced garlic
- 1 ½ tbsp minced ginger
- 4 scallions, cut into 2-inch lengths, then julienned
- 1 carrot, peeled and cut into 2-inch lengths, then julienned
- 2 tbsp Korean ground dried hot pepper
- ¼ cup cut strips of Asian pear

DIRECTION:

1. Prepare an ice bath, and bring a large pot of water to a boil. Submerge kale in boiling water and blanch for 3 minutes. Promptly remove the kale and transfer it to an ice bath. Once cool, drain the water and press the kale with your hands to remove as much water as possible. Toss kale with salt and set aside.
2. In a large bowl, combine water with sugar, and stir to dissolve. Add garlic, ginger, scallions, carrot, and ground hot pepper. Mix to combine. Add kale and Asian pear and stir until mixed well.
3. Pack tightly into a quart jar, pressing firmly as you go. Close the jar with a nonreactive lid and refrigerate for at least 4 hours before serving. Refrigerated, it will keep for around 7 days.

TRY INSTEAD: Asian pears have a mildly sweet flavor. If you don't have access to Asian pears, substitute a tart apple, which most closely resembles the flavor of this fruit.

92. Cucumber Kimchi

Preparation Time: 10 minutes
Cooking Time: 2 hours

INGREDIENTS:

- 3 Japanese cucumbers, thinly sliced
- 1 small tart apple, cored and thinly sliced
- 6 radishes, sliced
- 1 (1-inch) piece of ginger, peeled and sliced
- ½ lemon rind, grated on a Microplane grater
- 1 tsp Korean dried hot pepper powder
- ½ tsp salt
- 1 ½ tsp sugar
- 1 tbsp rice vinegar
- ¾ cup water

DIRECTION:

1. Mix cucumbers, the apple, radishes, ginger, and lemon rind in a nonreactive bowl. Add hot pepper powder, salt, sugar, and vinegar. Pour water over the kimchi. Cover the bowl and refrigerate for 2 hours before serving.

93. Pickled Ginger

Preparation Time: 10 minutes
Cooking Time: 3 to 6 days

INGREDIENTS:

- 2 cups water
- 1 tsp, plus ½ tsp salt, divided
- 3 oz ginger, peeled and thinly sliced
- ½ cup rice vinegar
- 2 tbsp sugar

DIRECTION:

1. In a pot, mix water and 1 tsp salt. Bring liquid to a boil and add ginger to the pot. Cook for 30 seconds and drain water.
2. Pack ginger into a sterilized jar.
3. Mix vinegar, sugar, and remaining ½ tsp salt in a nonreactive pot. Bring this liquid to a boil, remove it from heat, and allow it to come to room temperature.
4. Pour cooled liquid over the ginger, and store it refrigerated. It's best to eat after 2 to 3 days, but it will keep indefinitely.

94. Daikon in Soy Sauce

Preparation Time: 10 minutes
Cooking Time: 2 hours

INGREDIENTS:

- 1 lb daikon, peeled, cut lengthwise, and cut into half-moons
- 1 tsp pickling salt
- ½ lemon
- 3 tbsp soy sauce
- 1 tbsp mirin
- 1-inch piece kombu, cut into small pieces

DIRECTION:

1. Sprinkle daikon with salt, toss in a bowl, and allow to sit for 1 hour. Drain off any water.
2. Remove the rind from the lemon and dice rind finely. In a nonreactive bowl, mix soy sauce and mirin. Add lemon rind, kombu, and daikon, and mix well.
3. Cover the bowl with a small plate, and weigh down the plate using a large stone or jar filled with water. Halfway through curing time, mix seasoned daikon and weigh it down again. Serve after 1 or 2 hours.

Notes:

95. Garlic in Soy Sauce

Preparation Time: 10 minutes
Cooking Time: 2 months

INGREDIENTS:

- 5 to 6 whole garlic heads
- 1 cup rice vinegar
- ⅔ cup soy sauce
- 1 tbsp sugar

DIRECTION:

1. Peel only the outermost layer of skin from garlic heads. Trim away stems to allow you to pack garlic tightly.
2. Pack garlic into a sterile pint jar. Cover with vinegar, close the jar with a nonreactive lid and leave at room temperature for 2 weeks.
3. Strain vinegar off garlic, reserving vinegar. Measure ⅓ cup of reserved vinegar and mix it with soy sauce and sugar until sugar is dissolved. Pour this mixture over the garlic, cover with a nonreactive lid, and store the garlic refrigerated for at least 1 ½ months before eating. To serve, cut garlic heads diagonally through the head and serve each half whole.

A CLOSER LOOK: For pickles that will be refrigerated for a long time, or those prone to spoilage, a sterilized jar is called for to prevent the growth of mold, which can occur even when the pickle is refrigerated. To sterilize jars, simply boil them for 10 minutes before using them.

96. Miso Garlic

Preparation Time: 10 minutes
Cooking Time: 30 minutes

INGREDIENTS:

- 8 oz peeled garlic cloves
- 8 oz miso
- 3 tbsp mirin

DIRECTION:

1. Fill a small pot with water and bring it to a boil. Add garlic and cook for 2 minutes. Drain. Using a clean kitchen towel, pat cloves entirely dry.
2. Mix miso and mirin in a small bowl. Put about half of this mixture into the bottom of a pint jar. Place garlic cloves into the jar and cover them with the remaining miso paste mixture, pressing it down so that the cloves are well covered.
3. Cover the jar using a nonreactive lid, and refrigerate for at least 1 week before eating.

A CLOSER LOOK: There are several types of miso paste available, the most common being red and white miso. This pickle is typically made using red miso, which is stronger in flavor. However, it is perfectly fine to experiment with different types of miso paste. Try making these with your favorite variety and see what you think.

97. Takuan (Pickled Daikon)

Preparation Time: 10 minutes
Cooking Time: 1 to 3 months

INGREDIENTS:

- 2 lb daikon radish, preferably 2 or 3 thin and long ones
- ⅓ lb rice or wheat bran
- 4 tbsp pickling salt
- ½ tsp brown sugar
- 2 dried chili peppers, finely diced
- 1 (2-inch) square kombu, cut into several smaller pieces

DIRECTION:

1. Rinse daikon well, then hang outside in the sun, sheltered from rain, for 2 to 3 weeks. When daikon is easily bendable, they are ready for pickling.
2. Using your hands, roll the daikon on a cutting board to further soften the radish.
3. Mix bran, salt, brown sugar, and chili peppers in a bowl. Add ¼ of this mixture to the bottom of your pickling crock. Add half of the kombu to crock if you have 2 radishes, $1/3$ if you have 3 radishes. Layer the daikon into the crock, bending it so that it fits in the bottom of the crock. Cover radish with a layer of bran mixture. Add ½ or $1/3$ kombu, pack the next radish into the crock and then cover it with another portion of the bran mixture. If you have another radish, add it to the crock and use the remaining kombu and bran mixture to cover the daikon.
4. Place a small plate into the crock to cover the bran mixture, and cover the entire crock with a plastic bag. Place a heavy weight, around 4 to 6 pounds, on the plate to hold it down. Store crock in a cool location.
5. After 5 days, remove the weight and inspect the crock. If liquid has begun to rise, you can reduce weight to 2 pounds. If not, continue with heavier weight until the liquid rises.
6. After 1 month, remove the daikon, slice a piece, and taste it. If you like flavor, remove the daikon and eat it now. If not, let it continue pickling for up to 2 more months.

98. Spicy Pickled Daikon

Preparation Time: 10 minutes
Cooking Time: 3 to 6 days

INGREDIENTS:

- 1 lb daikon, peeled and cut into matchsticks
- 1 tsp salt
- 3 cloves garlic, minced
- 2 scallions, finely sliced
- 1 tsp toasted sesame seeds (see tip)
- 1 tbsp rice vinegar
- ½ tsp red chili pepper flakes
- 1 tsp sugar

DIRECTION:

1. Toss daikon with salt in a bowl and let sit for about 30 minutes. Drain the daikon and squeeze out any additional water using your hands.
2. Add remaining ingredients and mix well. Pack mixture into a pint jar and store for at least 2 hours before serving.

99. Eggplant Pickled in Soy Sauce

Preparation Time: 10 minutes
Cooking Time: 2 hours

INGREDIENTS:

- 4 Japanese eggplants
- 1 (4-inch) square kombu, cut into small shreds
- ¾ cup soy sauce
- 1 tbsp sake
- ½ tsp hot red chili pepper flakes

DIRECTION:

1. Halve eggplants lengthwise. Using a knife, make several small slits in the skin of eggplants. Transfer eggplants to a bowl and cover them with cold water. Soak for 30 minutes. Drain eggplants cut them into 1-inch pieces, and return them to the bowl.
2. Add remaining ingredients and stir to combine. Close the jar with a nonreactive lid and leave it at room temperature for 2 hours. Shake the jar occasionally during this time.
3. Take jar to refrigerator and store refrigerated for up to 1 week.

100. Quick-Pickled Cucumbers

Preparation Time: 10 minutes
Cooking Time: 12 hours

INGREDIENTS:

- 4 Asian-style pickling cucumbers
- 1 (2-inch) square kombu, cut into small strips
- 4 tbsp soy sauce
- 1 tbsp mirin

DIRECTION:

1. Wash and dry cucumbers and cut them into ½-inch-thick slices.
2. Rinse kombu and place it into a jar with cucumbers.
3. In a small bowl, mix soy sauce and mirin. Pour this mixture over the cucumbers and seal the jar using a nonreactive lid.
4. Refrigerate overnight, shaking the jar once or twice after mixing.

101. Pickled Cucumbers and Cabbage

Preparation Time: 10 minutes
Cooking Time: 3 hours

INGREDIENTS:

- 2 Japanese cucumbers
- 1 cup napa cabbage, cut into 2-inch pieces
- 1 tsp ginger, sliced
- 1 ½ tsp salt

DIRECTION:

1. Remove ends from cucumbers and discard. Slice cucumbers and mix them with cabbage, ginger, and salt.
2. Transfer the mixture to a wide-mouth jar, pressing firmly to fit it in the jar. Add a narrow, tall jelly jar filled with water and sealed to weigh it down.
3. Refrigerate cucumbers and cabbage, and serve within 3 hours.

102. Sweet Pickled Cucumbers

Preparation Time: 10 minutes
Cooking Time: 10 hours

INGREDIENTS:

- 4 Japanese pickling cucumbers
- 1 ⅓ tbsp pickling salt
- ½ cup water, divided
- 1 ¼ cups rice vinegar
- 3 tbsp sugar
- 1 dried chile pepper
- ½ tsp peppercorns

DIRECTION:

1. Wash cucumbers and trim both ends off. Cut cucumbers lengthwise and place them in a small dish where they can all lie relatively flat. Rub them with salt and pour ¼ cup of water over them. Cover cucumbers with a plate or other small dish to weigh them down, and leave them overnight or up to 24 hours at room temperature.
2. Rinse cucumbers under cool water and leave them in the open air until the surface is completely dry.
3. In a nonreactive pot, mix the remaining ingredients, including the remaining ¼ cup of water. Bring mixture to a boil, turn off the heat, and cool to room temperature.
4. Pack cucumbers into a pint jar, pressing them down tightly in the bottom. Pour cooled marinade over cucumbers. Close the jar with a nonreactive lid and refrigerate. Serve the following day, or store for up to 2 months.

103. Cucumber and Wakame Pickles

Preparation Time: 10 minutes
Cooking Time: 1 day

INGREDIENTS:

- 2 Japanese pickling cucumbers
- ½ cup sliced daikon
- 2 tbsp dried wakame
- ½ cup rice vinegar
- 1 (2-inch) square kombu, cut into 3 or 4 pieces
- 1 tsp pickling salt
- 1 tbsp sugar
- ¼ cup water

DIRECTION:

1. Pack prepared vegetables and wakame into a zip-top bag.
2. In a small nonreactive pot, combine the remaining ingredients and bring them to a boil, stirring to dissolve salt and sugar. Turn off the heat and bring the mixture to room temperature. Add this to the bag, seal it, and refrigerate for 12 to 24 hours. To serve, pour off the marinade. Eat pickles within 3 days of preparation.

Notes:

104. Pickled Cabbage

Preparation Time: 10 minutes
Cooking Time: 3 to 6 days

INGREDIENTS:

- ½ head cabbage (about 1 ¼ lb)
- 1 tbsp salt
- ½ cup water
- 1 (2-inch) square kombu, broken into 3 or 4 pieces
- 1 tbsp mirin

DIRECTION:

1. Cut cabbage into 3 wedges. In a nonreactive bowl, sprinkle each wedge with salt. Weigh the cabbage down, and pour ½ cup of water over the cabbage. Cover with a clean kitchen towel and leave at room temperature for 2 days.
2. Drain the cabbage and, using your hands, press out excess moisture. Place cabbage back into the bowl and add kombu. Pour mirin over the cabbage, cover the cabbage with a weight, and ferment for 3 days at room temperature. When slightly soured, transfer the cabbage to the refrigerator. Eat within 1 week of pickling.

105. Miso-Pickled Vegetables

Preparation Time: 10 minutes
Cooking Time: 1 day

INGREDIENTS:

- 1 lb celery, turnips, radish, daikon, or a combination, divided
- ½ cup miso paste
- 1 tbsp mirin
- 1 tbsp sake

DIRECTION:

1. Prepare vegetables by cutting them into small, thin pieces about ¼-inch thick.
2. Mix together miso paste with mirin and sake.
3. In a pint jar, spoon in about ¼ cup of miso paste mixture. Add vegetables, followed by ⅛ cup of miso mixture and the rest of the vegetables. Cover the top of the vegetables with the remaining ⅛ cup of miso mixture so that none are visible on top. Close the jar with a piece of plastic wrap and leave it at room temperature.
4. After 24 hours, take a vegetable out, rinse it off, and taste it. If it is to your liking, take pickles out. If not, leave for an additional 24 hours.
5. To serve, rinse pickles. These pickles are best within 24 hours of preparation, but they will keep for up to 3 days refrigerated. In between batches, store miso in the refrigerator.

Notes:

106. Chinese Fermented Mustard Greens

Preparation Time: 10 minutes
Cooking Time: 3 to 6 days

INGREDIENTS:

- 1 ½ lb mustard greens
- 2 tbsp pickling salt, divided
- ½ tsp Sichuan peppercorns
- 3 cups water

DIRECTION:

1. Wash mustard greens well and allow them to air-dry for about 12 hours, or until they begin to wilt.
2. In a bowl, combine mustard greens with 1 tbsp salt and peppercorns. Rub salt into greens and let them sit for 30 minutes until they begin to lose some water. Squeeze out as much of this water as possible, and transfer greens to a sanitized jar. Add the remaining 1 tbsp salt to the jar.
3. Bring water to a boil and pour it over the greens. Weigh down greens so that they are submerged in the jar. Cover the jar loosely with a nonreactive lid once the brine is cool, and store it in a room-temperature location.
4. After 10 days, greens will have taken on a bright green hue, signifying that they are finished. Remove the weight, close the jar tightly with a nonreactive lid, and transfer the jar to the refrigerator, where greens will keep for several months.

107. Daikon Kimchi

Preparation Time: 10 minutes
Cooking Time: 3 to 6 days

INGREDIENTS:

- 1 ¼ lb daikon, peeled and cut into 1-inch cubes
- 1 ½ tsp pickling salt
- 1 tbsp sugar
- 2 garlic cloves, minced
- 1 tbsp Korean ground dried hot pepper
- 2 scallions, cut into 1-inch pieces
- 1 (1-inch) piece of ginger, grated
- 1 tsp white vinegar

DIRECTION:

1. In a bowl, mix daikon, salt, and sugar. Let rest at room temperature for 30 minutes. Strain juice in the bowl, reserving it for later use.
2. Mix garlic, hot pepper, scallions, ginger, and vinegar together with daikon. Pack the mixture into a clean pint jar, pressing down firmly as you go to remove air bubbles. Pour reserved brine over radishes to cover. Cover the jar with a nonreactive lid, and leave kimchi at room temperature for 3 to 4 days. Take it to the refrigerator, where it will keep for several months.

Notes:

Chutneys, Salsas, and Relishes

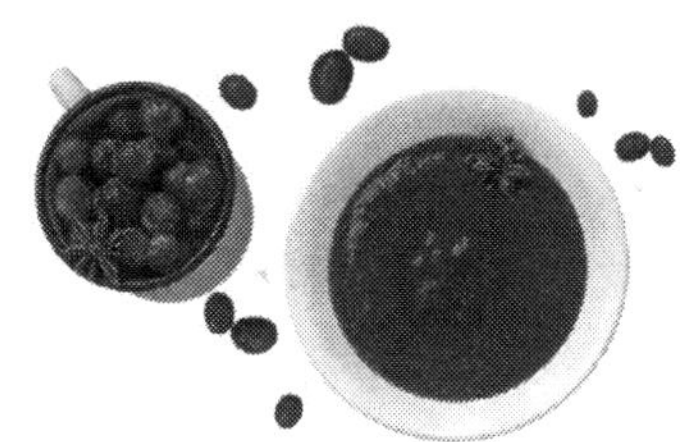

108. Plum Chutney

Preparation Time: 10 minutes
Cooking Time: 45 minutes

INGREDIENTS:

- ½ cup brown sugar
- ½ cup granulated sugar
- ½ cup white vinegar
- 1¾ cups purple plums, cored and chopped
- 2 tbsp chopped onion
- ½ cup golden raisins
- 1 tsp pickling salt
- 1 tsp mustard seeds
- 1 tbsp crystallized ginger
- 1 garlic clove, crushed
- ½ tsp red chili pepper flakes

DIRECTION:

1. In a nonreactive pot, combine sugars and vinegar and heat until simmering, stirring to dissolve sugars. Add all remaining fixings and stir well to mix. Bring the mixture to a boil and turn down the heat to a simmer. Cook for 45 minutes, until chutney, begins to thicken.
2. Ladle chutney into half-pint jars, leaving ¼ inch of headspace. Cap jars using two-piece canning lids.
3. Process chutney in a boiling-water bath for 10 minutes, or refrigerate.

109. Mango Chutney

Preparation Time: 10 minutes
Cooking Time: 65 minutes

INGREDIENTS:

- 2 mangos, ripe but not soft (see tip)
- 1 cup white vinegar
- 1 cup brown sugar
- 1 tsp hot pepper flakes
- ¼ tsp pickling salt
- 1½ tsp curry powder
- ¼ cup golden raisins

DIRECTION:

1. Mix all fixings except raisins in a bowl. Cover and allow to sit overnight at room temperature.
2. Next day, transfer the chutney to a nonreactive pot. Add raisins, bring mixture to a simmer, and cook until thickened, about 1 hour.
3. Ladle chutney into half-pint jars and cap using two-piece canning lids. Process for 10 minutes in a boiling-water bath or refrigerate.

110. Apple Chutney

Preparation Time: 10 minutes
Cooking Time: 45 minutes

INGREDIENTS:

- 2 cups chopped apples
- ¼ cup chopped onion
- ¼ cup chopped red bell pepper
- 2 hot red peppers, seeded and diced
- ½ cup golden raisins
- 1 cup brown sugar
- 1 tbsp ground ginger
- 2 tsp whole mustard seeds
- 2 tsp ground allspice
- ½ tsp pickling salt
- 1 garlic clove, minced
- 1 cup white vinegar

DIRECTION:

1. In a nonreactive pot, combine all ingredients. Boil the mixture, turn down the heat and simmer until thickened. Stir frequently as the chutney thickens to prevent scorching. It will take about 1 hour for the chutney to thicken.
2. Ladle hot chutney into two half-pint jars, leaving ½ inch of headspace. Cap jars with two-piece canning lids.
3. Process in a boiling-water bath for 10 minutes or refrigerate.

111. Lacto-Fermented Cranberry Chutney

Preparation Time: 10 minutes
Cooking Time: 2 days

INGREDIENTS:

- 1 lb fresh or frozen cranberries
- ½ cup honey
- 1 tsp sea salt
- ⅓ cup kombucha (non-pasteurized) or whey
- ½ cup white grape juice
- 1 tsp cinnamon
- Juice of 1 orange
- 2 tsp grated orange zest

DIRECTION:

1. Combine all ingredients except orange zest in a blender or food processor. Process until cranberries are well chopped, yet still chunky. Take the mixture to a quart jar and mix in orange zest.
2. Cover with a nonreactive lid and leave the jar at room temperature to ferment for 2 days. Transfer to refrigerator, where flavors will continue to develop.

Notes:

112. Lacto-Fermented Pineapple Chutney

Preparation Time: 10 minutes
Cooking Time: 2 to 3 days fermentation

INGREDIENTS:

- 1 pineapple, diced
- 1 bunch of cilantros, minced
- 1 (2-inch) piece of ginger, peeled and grated
- 2 tsp pickling salt
- Juice of 1 lime
- ½ cup kombucha (non-pasteurized) or whey
- ½ cup water

DIRECTION:

1. Mix pineapple, cilantro, ginger, and salt in a nonreactive bowl. Pack into a quart jar. Use a spoon to pack pineapple down into a jar, pressing to release some of its juices.
2. Mix together lime juice, kombucha, and water. Add mixture to a jar. Press pineapple into liquid, which should cover the chutney by about 1 inch. If it doesn't, add a bit more water until it does.
3. Cover the jar with a nonreactive lid, and leave it at room temperature to ferment for 2 to 3 days. Transfer the chutney to the refrigerator, where its flavors will continue to develop.

113. Pico De Gallo

Preparation Time: 10 minutes
Cooking Time: 0 minutes

INGREDIENTS:

- 1 lb ripe plum tomatoes, diced
- 1 tsp salt
- ½ white onion, peeled and diced
- 1 jalapeño pepper, seeds and stem removed, diced
- ¼ cup chopped cilantro leaves
- Juice of ½ lime

DIRECTION:

1. Toss tomatoes with salt, and drain for about 15 minutes.
2. Mix drained tomatoes with the rest of the ingredients. Refrigerate for up to 3 days.

Notes:

Alphabetical Recipe Index

Measurement Conversion Charts

VOLUME EQUIVALENTS (Liquid)		
US STANDARD	US STANDARD (OUNCES)	METRIC (APPROXIMATE)
2 tablespoons	1 fl. Oz.	30 ml
1/4 cup	2 fl. Oz.	60 ml
1/2 cup	4 fl. Oz.	120 ml
1 cup	8 fl. Oz.	240 ml
1 1/2 cups	12 fl. Oz.	355 ml
2 cups or 1 pint	16 fl. Oz.	473 ml
4 cups or 1 quart	32 fl. Oz.	947 ml
1 gallon	128 fl. Oz.	3,8 l

VOLUME EQUIVALENTS (Dry)	
US STANDARD	METRIC (APPROXIMATE)
1/8 teaspoon	0,5 ml
1/4 teaspoon	1 ml
1/2 teaspoon	2 ml
3/4 teaspoon	4 ml
1 teaspoon	5 ml
1 tablespoon	15 ml
1/4 cup	59 ml
1/3 cup	79 ml
1/2 cup	118 ml
2/3 cup	156 ml
3/4 cup	177 ml
1 cup	240 ml
2 cups or 1 pint	473 ml
3 cups	700 ml
4 cups or 1 quart	947 ml

WEIGHT	
IMPERIAL	METRIC
1/2 oz	15 g
1 oz	29 g
2 oz	57 g
3 oz	85 g
4 oz	113 g
5 oz	141 g
6 oz	170 g
8 oz	227 g
10 oz	283 g
12 oz	340 gr
13 oz	369 g
14 oz	397 g
15 oz	425 g
1 lb	453 g
1 1/2 lb	680 g
2,2 lb	1 kg

TEMPERATURE	
FAHRENHEIT	CELSIUS
5°	-15°
10°	-12°
25°	-4°
50°	10°
100°	37°
150°	65°
200°	93°
250°	121°
300°	150°
325°	160°
350°	180°
375°	190°
400°	200°
425°	220°
450°	230°
500°	260°

LENGTH		
INCHES	DECIMAL	MM
1/16	0,06	1,59
1/8	0,13	3,18
3/16	0,19	4,76
1/4	0,25	6,35
5/16	0,31	7,94
3/8	0,38	9,53
7/16	0,44	11,11
1/2	0,50	12,70
9/16	0,56	14,29
5/8	0,63	15,88
11/16	0,69	17,46
3/4	0,75	19,05
13/16	0,81	20,64
7/8	0,88	22,23
15/16	0,94	23,81
1	1,00	25,40

Made in the USA
Middletown, DE
14 December 2024